Austin M
TALKIN' YORKSHER

A compendium of all you need to know about God's Own County
but were too scared to ask.
Incorporating the Yorkshire Woman's Weekly (and how to get it)
Surviving in Yorkshire on ten words a Day
Beyond Barnsley: The Yorkshire Tourist Guide and
Teach Thissen Tyke: The Intelligent Southerner's Guide
to Yorkshire Language and Literature

Foreword by Richard Whiteley
Drawings by Stephen Abbey

GREAT NORTHERN

GREAT NORTHERN

GREAT NORTHERN BOOKS
Midland Chambers 1 Wells Road, Ilkley, LS29 9JB

© Text, Austin Mitchell 2002
© Illustrations, Stephen Abbey 2002
Printed by Amadeus Press Ltd, Bradford

ISBN: 0-9539740-4-9

Uniform with this volume:

Austin Mitchell's YORKSHIRE JOKES

British Cataloguing in Publication Data:
A catalogue for this book is available from the British Library

FOREWORD
BY RICHARD WHITELEY
FAMOUS YORKSHIRE PERSON

This has got to stop. "Never do a favour for a hopeless scrounger" was what my many friends told me when Austin Mitchell, a man who I hardly know anyway and would very much like to know less, asked me to write a brief preface for his pathetic collection of sexist, sordid, and politically very incorrect Yorkshire Jokes. "You'll be degraded by any association with that pathetic has been," or "Once you've given him something he'll be leaching on you forever" was what they said. Sadly, being the warm, impulsive, generous, person I am, I gave way, I cant bear to see grown men cry, so I wrote a rather wonderful, and certainly far too generous preface, for which I still haven`t been paid, though my golden words were almost certainly responsible for any sales his wretched effusions had. I hoped this would get rid of him. Preferably forever.

I WAS WRONG. He`s whinging for yet another preface to yet more of his maundering, maudlin, illiteracy, itself an illustration of how low educational standards were in the old Yorkshire he professes to love so much. I didn't see him personally. One can`t be sure where the wretched man has been in the thirty years since we so briefly worked together. Who knows what I might catch by even shaking hands with such a man. Someone constantly in the public eye and admired for my slim, elegant looks as I am, couldn`t afford to take the risk. However he continued to bombard me with begging letters which, after they'd been appropriately fumigated, I read, as I do all the thousands of loving letters I receive every day. After seeking advice from my accountant, my lawyer, my business manager, my dresser, the manager of my sensational website (www.superwhiteley.com), I finally relented, though they'd told me not to. To a woman. I am very widely recognised as an equal opportunity employer. Why, apart from that natural generosity which inclines me to do anything for a fee, did I take on such a damaging, unrewarding and tasteless commitment as dignifying these pathetic scribblings by a few well crafted words from one of Yorkshire's greatest writers?

One doesn`t have to like people one works with – though I find that everyone I work with likes me. So to stop this stream of requests for my brilliant prefaces to his rubbishy books, let me say here that I never really liked Mitchell. Nobody much does and they not much. Yet I do feel that I have a responsibility to protect Yorkshire from its more base instincts, namely him.

He is a boil on the Yorkshire bottom, and the left buttock at that, whereas I am in all modestly the Greatest Living Yorkshireman, natural heir to such previous contenders for that title as J. B. Priestley, Wilfred Pickles and James Mason, even though none was as well known as I am. So I have an enormous responsibility to our county. I am revered by its people, patron to many of its most important organisations, clubs and societies, and I patronise its citizens too. So I must speak for the real Yorkshire, the Yorkshire in which I have my being and spend most of my waking hours doing Channel Four's most successful programme Countdown. My Yorkshire is the exciting New Yorkshire of art, literature, high culture, fashion and style, Gourmet Yorkshire, and the higher aspects of life to which I make such an important contribution. As one of the most important figures of this New

Yorkshire and, indeed, its driving force, I must protect all that's best about our county from Mitchell's sad and mendacious attempt to portray such a progressive, sophisticated, world as the fish and chip guzzling, Tetley's slurping, dialect shouting, in your face, yob county he describes.

New Century, New Yorkshire, with a glittering future which I embody. Mitchell's view isn't even accurate on Yorkshire's past. I would regularly point that out to him when he was last usefully employed, which is three decades ago. His sad scribblings are a slur of a type which could only be written by a pathetic failure like him though perhaps a county which produced two such sharply contrasting people as myself and Mitchell is Manichean. I can only be described as High Yorkshire, like the Brontes, Priestley, Hockney and, possibly, Ashley Jackson, several of whose paintings I own. Mitchell wallows in Low Yorkshire, pathetically unable, as Virgil would have put it, to ascencare ad super aes as I have so successfully done.

So I write this preface to give the real, the honest, the elegant picture of the best Yorkshire, the world in which I move. I have the responsibility to defend and describe that better world. Like me, it's highly educated with my programmes regularly shown at the Bradford Museum of photography and television (which, shows the Best of Countdown ie. every edition, of this, the world's most popular and longest running television programme). Indeed, my personal papers are now being transferred to my alma mater, Cambridge University, to form the nucleus of the Richard Whiteley Studies course, shortly to be offered as the most interesting part of Modern Greats.

Such recognition is richly deserved, yet Mitchell is unable to see that it is in response to strongly felt public wishes and has become more than usually jealous. Having heard that the University of York is embarking on a Yorkshire Studies course in which my own writing, work and oeuvre will play a major part, Mitchell is hoping that his booklets will be prescribed when they should be proscribed. The large number of students anxious to learn about me should not fork out good money for what they might be deceived into thinking is a text book. Save your money, disciples. You'll learn nothing from Mitchell. Far better to turn to the various books by Joan Ingilby and Marie Hartley on life and tradition in the various Ridings, of WR (Bill), the far better Mitchell or, moving up to my own level, the works by my friends, Lords Hattersley and Healey, on their Yorkshire boyhoods, or my own account of my own fascinating childhood, *Preparation for Greatness:The Baildon Years* (forthcoming). This book will, in all due modesty, be widely recognised as seminal. Mitchell's more pathetic production is merely stained with it, although the publishers are trying to make amends with my glorious new book *Richard Whiteley's Yorkshire Quiz* (also forthcoming).

It's time for the world to know that there is a New Yorkshire, a dynamic and exciting society, to which I, in all due modesty, have played a prominent part in shaping, acculturating and building. It bears no resemblance at all to the grimy, grubby, clapped out world Mitchell both writes about in his grubby, clapped out way, and exemplifies. Indeed that world was out of date in the l960s when Mitchell tried to persuade us on my programme, *Calendar*, to do a series of films on such things as Knurr and Spell, Tip-cat, Tipsy (apparently the result of playing Knurr and Spell at the Springrock Inn , Elland), Nipsy, Progging, all unknown to me but which Mitchell claimed to have played to Olympic levels in his youth when I knew for a fact the only thing he'd played then was truant.

He loved to make films on Pit, Mill and Bug oil closures and on so called traditional figures in the Yorkshire Dales, most of whom turned out to be incurable alcoholics. All these so called "ideas", which he appeared to have read in a nineteenth century book about dialect from which he was practising his Yorkshire accent after years in New Zealand, were naturally greeted with derision by my *Calendar* team. Fortunately they are now lost from the archives after being expensively filmed in remote Dales pubs which appeared on checking not to exist.

No! What Mitchell doesn't make clear, so I must, is that a Yorkshire Phoenix has risen from the ashes of the old. This is a New Yorkshire of digital technology, computer chips, stylish chaps like me, and chapesses who, like me, embody high-tech, urbane elegance, the very glass of fashion and the mould of form, as one reviewer described my specially tailored apparel for Countdown. Yorkshire is the future, Mitchell past tense. The rest of us, hopefully without him, are moving forward with Yorkshire Forward. Mitchell and the few geriatrics and Luddites who think like him are desperate to drag it back because they cant bear to admit that their day has gone. If it was ever here in the first place.

Mitchell, in short, is fighting the dead battles of the past, usually in defence of his own failed career. The rest of us are moving onto the sunlit uplands of the New Yorkshire. Mitchell would relegate us to the world of back-to-backs and outside lavatories, a particularly appalling fate for women who in his world would be condemned to spend their lives putting yellow pumice stone on their door steps, turning mangles and possing in the peggy-tub instead of appearing with me in Yorkshire Life or becoming famous as hostesses on my TV shows.

So my purpose in agreeing to pen this preface, the last I will ever do for him, is not so much a Government Health, as a Mental Health, Warning about the author and the corrosive effects of his crude, insensitive, views. All are the antithesis of how right thinking Yorkshire folk view their county. The danger is that if such views are taken seriously outside Yorkshire we will simply be dismissed as a race of boors, boozers and the generally unrefined. Like Mitchell. I am not prepared to have my County slurred like his speech.

Sitting here in my personally contoured Conran leather armchair, giving myself the pleasure of watching my world famous interview with the Ferret which bit me (a video I have on continuous loop and play regularly to my friends because it reminds me so much of dealing with Mitchell) while drinking a fine brandy and re-reading my brilliant Foreword before it goes to the poor sucker of a publisher Mitchell has inflicted himself on, I am inclined to suggest that mine, being not so much the best part of the book as the only part that's worth reading at all, your best course, dear reader, is to erase the name Mitchell from the cover, underline mine and tear out all the contents, apart from this Preface. Then Mitchell's out of date and offensive view of my county won`t pollute either your book shelf or, in all due modesty, one of the best things ever written about Yorkshire: this preface.

Alternatively, for cash conscious Yorkshire readers who feel disinclined to chuck anything away once they've paid for it, even failed lottery tickets, I have another suggestion. If you've bought the book, paid cash for it (I have a Platinum card, of course, and don't touch money) and then been upset that it's not suitable for colouring, let me tell you how to treat it and post a warning, not of its many failures and inaccuracies of detail but of why its broad approach is fundamentally flawed and deeply damaging to the real interests of a county which is still the best in the land, despite Mitchell.

So here`s a short and, I`m sure, welcome guide through the swamps, the nostalgie de la boue, as we used to call it at Giggleswick, which Mitchell is so happy to wallow in like a blind, an E.S.N. and a rather smelly hippopotamus. In biblical exegesis my comments would be called a Concordance at Baildon Weslyans. But Mitchell's work is far from divine. Taking it chapter by chapter I'd say:-

Chapter One The superlatives about Yorkshire are mostly correct though for some reason they fail to include me. The are also clamorously overstated. A genuine Yorkshireman would cut out the hype and opt for understatement but Mitchell over-eggs the Yorkshire pudding, probably because he`s never made one, possibly because of a deep and well justified insecurity about whether Yorkshire folk can stand him.

Chapter Two This history is a travesty of our county's glorious past. History was clearly not taught at Woodbottom Council School. Along with manners, etiquette, charm, and preparation for the world of work as distinct from scrounging. Having been educated at Gigglesick I am trained to recognise a load of crap when I see it.

Chapter Three The Language. Given the social divide in Baildon between Top Baildoners, the elite, and Lower Baildoners, the hewers of wood and drawers of water, it is natural that there should be difference of language. We at the top, living a life style immortalised by John Braine, and speaking like Wilfred Pickles or Sir Marcus Fox, were more elegant. Those lower down, and Mitchell right at the bottom, were more broad, in accent and bottom. It is totally unnecessary to speak dialect in Harvey Nicholls, or Harrogate, or anywhere where I am seen. So I recommend sensitive readers to skip this part of the book. Along with the rest. Avoid trying to flaunt working class backgrounds you don't have or forcing your unpleasant experiences in outside lavatories on us. We know it's a pose and I am surprised Mitchell has failed to grasp that lowly backgrounds like his are no longer necessary. They`re a positive disadvantage, particularly in today's Labour Party where he has been so completely relegated. Indeed, he`s recognised as incapable of even making a cup of tea, let alone intelligent conversation.

Chapter Four How to be a Yorkshireman is the perfect formula for career failure both in Yorkshire and outside. It goes a long way to explaining the mess Mitchell has made of his own. It is not necessary today to hate and despise Southerners as Mitchell does. It could even give rise to race relations charges. Some of my best friends are from the South and they admire me immensely. I never speak in dialect to anyone, except perhaps a few poor workers on my estate. As a public school chap I was educated to be at ease with all social types, even the lowest, and being egalitarian I`ll talk down to anyone, but never in dialect. This training failed in my, fortunately, brief relationship with Mitchell. Yet it has been sufficient to ensure that I am adored in the South almost as much as within the Broad Acres, even South Yorkshire. Mitchell' s anti-Southernism makes me wonder if he is trying to whip up Yorkshire nationalism to get himself elected to some Yorkshire Assembly in yet another pathetic attempt to rescue something from the ruins of his political career. It cuts no ice with me. It won`t with New Yorkshire.

Chapter Five Conclusion. My objections to this are similar, though alloyed with relief that it is the end of this pathetic rhodomontade, a book of which the publishers, printers, editors, booksellers and purchasers should all be deeply ashamed, though I know well that Mitchell won`t be. He hasn't the sensitivity, the intelligence or the integrity to feel such emotion.

Don't think in rejecting Mitchell's maudlin view of a Yorkshire that never was that I never knew the old Yorkshire he tries to identify with. I remember its sights, its smells, its hawking and spitting, mostly emanating from Mitchell. I remember the days when the maimed were condemned to sell matches and recycled back numbers of *Tit Bits* and when every village had its village idiot, a post Mitchell himself applied for in our home village of Baildon, looking forward to standing around Towngate drooling and shouting. He was assessed as being of insufficient intelligence for the job so he just stood around drooling and shouting anyway.

Forget his past. Look to our future. Yorkshire people are as proud of their county as they are of me. But they don't want to play Mitchell's game of "more working class than thou" or of "our outside lavatory was further away from the house than yours". Who cares? Yorkshire has been sandblasted, rebuilt, cleaned up and modernised. Most Yorkshire folk would never dream of saying "Nathen Thee", and neither would I in my frequent meetings with the Queen and the Lord Lieutenant of North Yorkshire in my capacity as the most popular Mayor Wetwang has ever had.

The past has been pulled down. It deserved to be. Mitchell observes that his past has been pulled down too. He should have been as well. Many years ago. That being the nicest thing I can find to say about this pathetic rubbish, it provides a good and welcome note on which to end my rather well written Preface. Which I hope will have been of some small service in demonstrating that there is a real, a good, a New Yorkshire which is so much better than Mitchell's maungy maunderings.

One final word (as I say on Countdown). None of what I say about Mitchell applies to his long suffering and much better half who is charming, lovely, gifted and writes like an angel being, in short, the complete antithesis of the man she has the misfortune to be married to. Frankly, I don't know how she puts up with him, his asinine views and his braying declamation of them. I'd dedicate this Foreword to her as a Yorkshire Martyr. If I could remember her name.

Richard Whiteley
Mayor of Wetwang
Yorkshireperson Extraordinary
Friend of the Great and of the People Alike

'OO DOES AUSTIN MITCHELL THINK HE USED TO BE?

Austin Mitchell usually. In the long ago days when he used to be asked for his autograph because he had been seen with Richard Whiteley he would take a macabre pleasure in signing as "Alderman Mitchell, Mayor of Heckmondwike 1893-4," or even "Stanislaus Poniatowski, former King of Poland," laughing heartily in his Basil Brush fashion while baffled incomprehension crossed the faces of the young Yorkshire innocents who'd asked for his autograph under the mistaken impression that he was someone of interest or importance.

Austin Mitchell laughing heartily in his Basil Brush fashion while baffled incomprehension crosses the face of the young Yorkshire innocents who'd asked for his autograph.

He is. Because he's a true Yorkshireman, having been conceived one Baildon Tide week, a festival since abolished because of this. He grew up in Baildon where Richard Whiteley looked down on him from the heights of Upper Baildon, immortalised by John Braine in *Room at the Top*. He variously claims to be descended by an illegitimate line from John Hartley, the famous Yorkshire poet and alcoholic. He has had articles rejected by the *Yorkshire Post, the Yorkshire Journal, the Dalesman, Yorkshire Life, Yorkshire Ridings Magazine* and the *Daily Sport*. Usually on grounds of taste.

Now he lives in semi-retirement up a nick i'Bowling, down Carr Lane, where he went to hide after the police discovered that his Youth for Yorkshire camps at Appletreewick only admitted nubile young girls with large fronts and comfortable bottoms. The poor, innocent girls were forced to spend the week stark naked singing "On Ilkla Moor Baht Bra" while being lightly flagellated by Mitchell. Parents complained and the camps were closed down, though Mitchell was too exhausted to give evidence against himself and declined to speak in court at all unless he could do so in Broad Dialect.

The police discovered that Austin Mitchell's Youth for Yorkshire camps only admitted nubile young girls who were forced to spend the week singing "On Ilkla Moor Baht Bra".

He now awaits the creation of an elected Parliament for Yorkshire for which he intends to stand on a "Home Rule and Summat Besides" ticket. John Prescott and the people of Yorkshire have other ideas. Unlike most Yorkshire folk he is not as nice as he looks. Particularly on Wednesdays.

WELCOME TO GOD'S OWN COUNTY

No-one else is going to say it to you because, frankly, you're not. It would be nicer if you'd just sent us your money instead of coming in person to litter our lovely county, over-stretch our resources and push up our prices, particularly in the Dales and around Holmfirth. Being Yorkshire we like the money (brass it's called round here and it has a great religious significance) but you, coming from the South, we're none too keen on. "Guilty until proved innocent" is the best verdict you're likely to get.

So we make it difficult for folk to come up to discover the source of the M1 and GNER makes it so expensive by train that you have to take out a mortgage. We don't want a lot of rag, tag and yobtail. So the points of entry, Doncaster station, Darlington, the huge traffic jams on the M62 as folk flee from Lancashire and Eckingron Service Station on the MI, are the most unpleasant parts of Yorkshire - crowded, smelly and usually crammed with returning football fans and other drunks vomiting in celebration of triumphs south of the border, down Birmingham way. Worse still, is an arrival in Leeds in the rush hour, or via Leeds station which has been closed for two years, all to put off people like you.

Don't rush to Harrogate for safety, or dash straight to the Dales. Work your way up from bottom dale to top: starting with the mucky ones, Don (dirty flows the Don) Calder (unclean the Calder), then on to Aire, Wharfe, Nidd, Ure, and Swale where the shopping trolleys and the dead dogs run out. But first acclimatise in Doncaster or, if you came up the M1, Rotherham. Buy some fish and chips. Ask for the upmarket premium package wrapped in the *Yorkshire Post*. Walk round town offering them to people but on no account offer them money. This is Doncaster, and some may be councillors. Go into a pub and order drinks all round. It won't be a big bill because most will die of shock. Call no one "my good man" and certainly not "my good lady". The ones you're likely to meet at this time of night aren't. Pretend to be dumb. Say nothing, but murmur appreciatively at anything people say to you. Unless it's "Oy, tha's` spilled mi bloody beer" in which case practice walking backwards to avoid what could be a fecal, even a fatal, accident.

Then go back to your bedroom and read, learn and digest this Compendium of How to Survive in Yorkshire. Practice the hard consonants and the short vowel sounds, but not to the extent that people in the next room think you're having sex. That will make them listen all night to ensure you're treating women properly. Learn the following rules on how to behave in Yorkshire.

RULES FOR SURVIVAL IN YORKSHIRE

RULE ONE – Don`t Expect A Welcome

We're not the welcoming sort. We`re doing you a favour by letting you in and that`s enough. So don`t expect Yorkshire waiters to give you a little welcoming speech. "`Ello. I'm Herbert Clogworthy, tha waiter for ter neet. We've got nowt much for thi but t'black pudden's noan so bad. If there's any left for thee".

"Ello, I'm Herbert Clogworthy, tha waiter for ter neet."

No need to welcome you. You've arrived in God's Own County, the most beautiful in Britain, and probably the world. That`s enough. Not quite paradise - we haven`t got regional government yet - but certainly twinned with Paradise and the most beautiful, biggest and the best country. We're different to the rest and different means better. If Yorkshire-folk have one fault it`s modesty. They never blow their own trumpet and it takes a couple of minutes and as many drinks before they can be persuaded to admit that Yorkshire is the best of counties. Almost too good for this world. Which is why its so far away from it.

Don't criticise it or act superior. You're definitely not. Uphimselfism, though anatomically difficult, is a crime in Yorkshire. Nor should you make jokes about

Yorkshire folk. Let your indulgent smile turn into a laugh, imply in any way that they do things better down south or that it has any advantages over us except proximity to the Royal Family and we're not bothered about that, since they dumped Princess Ferguson on us, and blood will flow. Your`s. You'll get the ritual excommunication. "If you don't like it why don`t you bugger off? We didn't ask you to come". That`s the end. Ignorance of the lore is no excuse.

RULE TWO – Praise Yorkshire
Not too lavishly unless you`ve got the politician`s skill of faking sincerity. Nor do we expect you to sing Yorkshire's praises for quite as long as us. We know Yorkshire. You don`t. As a county Yorkshire has one major preoccupation. Yorkshire. The rest of the country ignores us, until it`s thumped. We don`t ask "What do you think of Yorkshire then?" a hundred times before you`ve even got off the train because we know you`ve no alternative to liking it. But say so frequently and say nothing critical if you value your teeth. You walk a delicate tightrope avoiding culture shock while not upsetting the natives who easily get violent.

RULE THREE – Read All About Us
Paul Theroux never visited. Most travel writers stay away, probably because they re all poufters, cultural snobs or other perverts who're not welcome. Bill Bryson lived here but never dared write about us because the degree of praise necessary wasn't in his vocabulary. Raymond Postgate never sampled Bert's Diner on the A1 to confer three stars on its egg on toast, none on its Egon Ronay. The author of *See Europe on Five Dollars a Day* stayed for a year in the Salvation Army hostel in Hull until treated for alcoholism. Michael Winner ventured to the border but then turned round thinking Yorkshire was closed. Good riddance.

Yorkshire folk are neither demonstrative nor articulate. These are signs of effeminacy. As John Prescott puts it "Some folk is eloquent and some the gift of the gab not have". Some can however, write a bit. Like Fred Trueman on Aesthetics, Dicky Bird on ornithology, Arthur Scargill on industrial relations, John Prescott on boxing, the *Yorkshire Post* on Socialism, Jude Kelly on Rugby and Ashley Jackson on strip clubs. The purpose of these books is therapeutic, not diagnostic, a re-assurance industry. So carry one with your everywhere. Preferably this.

You`ll never wade through the books of colour photographs of Yorkshire, the Dales, its canals, cricket grounds or public toilets. Producing them is a major local industry second only to making fake miners` lanterns and coal statues of Arthur Scargill. Books on Denis Healey's Dales pour out from any printers unlucky enough not to get the Gala Bingo account. Their sale is not encouraged outside the Broad Acres least they bring too many people here. Jumbo jets would pour into Yeadon, Humberside and, if it ever opens, Doncaster. Coaches would tour the working men`s clubs where the strippers' ripping velcro and the howling of the Karaoke would be drowned by a thousand video cameras. Remaining miners' baths, like those of the rugby clubs, would be on public display and re-enactments of native courting habits in the back of parked cars on the moors a major attraction. We don't want that. So this is your best, indeed only, guide to the wonderful world of the Broad Acres. Now with added Humberside.

Re-enactments of native courting habits in the back of parked cars.

RULE FOUR –Conform or Die

Tykes are hard men and not very soft women. Men are men, and women glad of it. Often. Impotence is unknown except in Harrogate. Viagra was invented for Southerners. We have Websters. Life is hard in God's Own County, its denizens harder still. So you're at risk of a friendly butt in the face, or a heart warming kick in the balls when you come "up" (notice that its up not "down") to Yorkshire. We are the apogee, the heights, to be looked up to by the South. Don't presume on our hospitality for too long. You have to conform and quickly. So gerronwiit. Or Gerrout. The train back to London leaves Doncaster from Platform I or 3. The bus is cheaper but may be full of Yorkshire folk heading South in a vengeful mood. As soon as you pass the sign erected when Geoff Boycott announced that he was going to live in the South, "You are now leaving Yorkshire. You Great Nance" you'll feel twinges of regret because it applies to you. You've failed the Great Yorkshire Outward Bound Course. You'll always be marked down as a wimp and probable pansy and in your heart you'll know you are. So mi old flower, read mi Vade Theecum an tha'll be reet.

Your aim should be to visit the Broad Acres, the best part of the civilised world, and there make yourself understood to humanity's finest flowering: Yorkshire folk. You'll encounter them in large numbers, sometimes physically, occasionally verbally, but always to your advantage. This book will allow you to communicate with them to the limited extent necessary to understand how wonderful they are. It won't bring mastery of the language but its use will stop you being laughed at, mimicked, or enduring pain. This is not a Yorkophone course bringing mastery in days, naturalisation in months, but it will inculcate the essentials and allow you to conform to the Norm. And to Fred

RULE FIVE – Commune in Silence

Don`t speak until you`re spoken to. If folk say nowt it`s because you're not worth it. If they don't reply to your questions it`s because there's no need. Never assume they`re stupid or even dead. They`re weighing you up and will reach a pretty accurate verdict. They'll treat you at you're worth, not in accord with your status, education, class or dignity. Southerners all think their shit doesn`t stink, Tykes know it does. Even ours – a bit. That`s why we have outside lavatories.

All you ever need to say is, "This must surely be the loveliest county in the whole world".

All you ever need to say is, " This must surely be the loveliest county in the whole world". You'll get an enthusiastic "Appen so", meaning that`s bloody obvious. So it is with attractions Tykes will list at the drop of a cheque, the best golden beaches made nicer by global warming, the Dales which Turner would regularly rush North to paint, the hills and moors whereas Lancashire is all mills and ......well, nothing comparable. The moors have inspired some of Britain's best photographers and painters. Indeed Ashley Jackson developed the technique of doing moor paintings on his cheques, so no one cashed them. When Air Yorkshire offered In-flight Yorkshire Puddings - themselves lighter than air - it quickly went bankrupt. There's nowhere nicer outside Yorkshire to fly to.

RULE SIX – Recognise Their Greatness

Yorkshire folk are proud because Yorkshire is the biggest and they're the best. The East Riding Eugenics Institute tells us our genes are better, and Tykes have more space per capita per bum to grow bigger, taller, better and fitter. The overcrowded South stunts like battery hens but this the Big County. Biggest mills, biggest mines, biggest fish and chip shops, biggest trouser bottoms and bums, biggest chimneys, biggest heads, biggest acreage, biggest whores, biggest drawers. That's Yorkshire.

Yorkshire has won the County Cricket Championships more than any other, was the birthplace of the founder of socialism, Robin Hood of Britain's best politicians, Lord Rockingham, Herbert Asquith, Harold Wilson, Denis Healey, Arthur Scargill of its finest poet John Hartley, its great authors, though their names temporarily escape me, except for those named after places like Barbara Taylor Bradford-Moor and Phyllis Bentley-Colliery, its greatest actors, such as James Mason of Huddersfield, Sooty from Bradford and Arnold Thumplugs of the Drighlington Allotments Society, its most proficient mass murderers, Christie, Neilson and Sutcliffe, (the subject of my own blank verse poem "Doin'Owt Toneet"), its greatest astronomer, Fred Hoyle, (a distinguished product, though sadly the only one of Bingley Grammar School), its best cricketers, Fred Truman, Geoff Boycott, Len Hutton, Herbert Sutcliff, Darren Gough, its finest painter, David Hockney. Everything is bigger and better. John Poulson gave us Britain's biggest corruption scandal, Doncaster its biggest council bribery with 20 arrested. So far.

All this is chronicled by the Yorkshire Society, a distinguished body of Tykes devoted to the quiet pleasure of onanism and contemplating their county's greatness, because they're too old for sex. The finest scenery, the most dry stone walls (climbing cliffs, which would have terrified Edmund Hillary just to show who belongs them) the most awkward buggers, the greatest mileage of tarmac, the most extensive working railways (as distinct from those run by Railtrack) the least polluted atmosphere and the best fish and chip shops. Indeed chips would now be called "Yorkshire Fries" had Harry Ramsden patented them, but being a true Yorkshireman he wouldn't fork out the two and ninepence necessary so the Frogs grabbed it.

In short, we're Cock of the North and even better with Eckington and South Humberside, Yorkshire's Gateway to Europe, added in. As J.B. Priestlety put it, "We're bloody marvellous. All on us. Me, an even thee. But particularly me". The proudest.

RULE SEVEN – Don`t Insult Us
Never ask someone if he's a Yorkshireman. If he is he'll tell you so proudly in the first twenty seconds with frequent repeats thereafter just in case you haven`t registered your wonderment at his good fortune. If he isn't then why humiliate him by asking? Don't express any criticism of him, his family, other Tykes or his county. He doesn't want you to make a fool of yourself and have to be corrected physically rather than by any long explanation of the obvious. Listen in admiration, occasionally saying "Bloody Ummer" or "Tha`s reet". This process is known as conversation.

RULE EIGHT – Understand the Tyke
The Yorkshireman is a man of few words. Most of those are "bugger off". A natural loner, he prefers his own company because it`s the best around, and enjoys it on his allotment or in his shed. Where Americans jog and the Chinese do Tai (or is it Lai) Chee, he sits and stares. Sometimes he just sits. He's conservative so Yorkshire votes Labour and not given to chatter, charm, courting, creeping, counselling, or conciliating. The Labour Party gave up running focus groups in Yorkshire.They just sat there in sullen silence picking their noses producing amazing discoveries but not the ones the Party wanted.

He's a good hater with an elephant's memory for feuds. Look at the way old cricketing codgers carry on vendettas arising from some obscure incident on the 1958 tour of Australia. Heathcliffe was a typical Tyke though smuggled in under plain cover from Lancashire. The feuds of the Crowthers of Bankdam pale into insignificance against the murderous vendettas of the Wool Barons and the Wars of the Roses are still going on after 600 years. He likes dogs, preferably big ones, not the yappy Terrier which, so inexplicably bears his name. That's small, fussy, temperamental, and prone to pee all over the place. Totally unlike him. He doesn't use psychologists or public relations advisers. He is what he is. Like it or lump it. Though if you don`t like you get the lump.

RULE NINE – Yorkshire Folk are Born not Made
You will eventually become such an admirer you`ll want to become a Yorkshireman. You can`t. The lists have closed. Except for those with patriality from parents or grandparents who are Tykes and preferably worked down a mine or in a mill. Being born here is essential. When it was necessary to play for the cricket team, the M1 was thronging with proud dads driving pregnant wives over the border in time for the baby to be born a true Tyke, though in case of doubt selectors could extend the border as they did by one bedroom for Fred Trueman in Maltby. Alternatively the place of conception could be taken in to account to discourage playing away. Now the requirement has been abandoned for playing though not for commentating on the club, the county, or anything pertaining to either. Don't stick your own fillings in or you'll lose yours.

Associate county status is available to those who live here for more than twenty years and master these rules and frequent visitor status to all who express contrition for being born elsewhere and drink specified quantities of Theakston's "Lunatic" brew. Finally, you could marry into us. Yorkshire women are house-trained and nicer than the men, though a few liberationists have hidden in Harrogate. Otherwise read this book. Do the exercises. Hear no evil, see no evil and speak no evil about Yorkshire. And hope. You might make it one day.

US HISTORY: COPULATION AS A WAY OF YORKSHIRE LIFE

Yorkshire was the cradle of civilisation long before Homo Australopithecus Africanus emerged 2.8 million years ago. He was almost certainly moving towards Yorkshire, but too slowly to make it. Neanderthals merged with Homo Erectus, or Stringfellow Man, 0.3 million years ago. Homo Sapiens, also known as Tykonian Man was the first Yorkshiremen to stand so tall their knuckles didn't reach the floor. He evolved on Ilkla Moor baht'at (or owt else for that matter) 200,000 years ago. Like the best products, Yorkshire folk took time but there was pleasure in the procreation process.

All this has been established by archaeological work carried out by the National Coal Board (R.I.P). Deep seams have yielded fossils, bones and food remnants indicating that Yorkshire was the cradle of civilisation before anything on the Euphrates. Before crops were cultivated there Yorkshire had dry stone walls to prevent sheep being sexually interfered with so that human evolution could go on without unnecessary distractions.

This research has now been written up by Albert Gaukroger, Professor of Archaeology, Prehistory and Deep Fat Frying at the College of Tetley Technology (P.C.W. Provident Cheques Welcome) in Heckmondwike (just before the Mason's Arms). Gaukroger was man of few words, particularly on Mondays, Wednesdays and Fridays, when Alcoholics Anonymous didn't meet. Most of those words were terse and unprintable though fortunately his publications are numerous, if a little beer-stained. A few even bear the traces of grease, evocative of the research for his narrative poem "Land of a Thousand Chip Oils".

Gaukroger's publications are as well written as a Harry Ramsden's menu and supplemented by his website, Nathen Thee, with an address frequently confused with that of French Connection UK. Collected with his obiter dicta on the backs of betting slips the, Gaukroger legacy makes Yorkshire's key role in the development of civilisation clear. Even to people from Essex.

Tykonian Man, or Homo Tykoniensis, a name he rightly objected to at the time, arrived in the first (pre-Bird's Eye) Ice Age when the climate was deteriorating faster than Filey on a wet Wednesday. He would have been able to walk here, even had the North Sea been full of water. Except that it wasn't for Britain was still connected to Europe by land, an unpleasant and debilitating association which God took immediate steps to dissolve just as soon as his western Garden of Eden, Yorkshire, had been sufficiently populated by the finest stock then available. He then pulled the North Sea plug and retired from direct intervention in the world, content that Yorkshiremen were now there, designed on his plan, shaped by his hand, and ready always to do his work because they knew his mind so well, were now in their heaven.

The world was cut off from Yorkshire as unworthy, though if the North Sea gets any more polluted Yorkshirefolk may soon be able to walk back again. No damage there because it's cheaper than the ferry and could facilitate our civilising mission in Europe, but a real problem if other lesser breeds without the county, Frogs, Krauts, or Belchums, began to come the other way breaching the North Sea defences which, as the Yorkshire poet once observed, have served proud Yorkshire as a moat or a bloody great version of the Leeds and Liverpool canal.

The language of Tykonian Man was probably Indo European but then as now much communication was in the form of grunts and low moans. Only one word has survived in such place names as Eckington, Heckmondwike or simply Heck, indicating that "Heck", or "Bloody Heck", was Tykonian Man`s cry on glimpsing this C&IU affiliated version of paradise. `Eck is not to be confused with Ecce Homo. That`s Latin and later, and means I have certain suspicions of this person. Nor with "By `Eck" which is a religious exclamation sworn by Saint Heck, Yorkshire's patron saint.

We can only conjecture what life was like in the very first Tykonian settlements in this second Garden of Eden. We can, however, be sure that since this remains a paternalist, male dominated, society, Tykonian Man wasn't going to listen to any daft ideas from Tykonoian Mrs which might get them both expelled, so the recreations of the parochial scenes by nineteenth century painters, whose efforts are in Leeds City Art Gallery, are patently false showing huge muscled, powerful figures which is right, but arriving by ship, which is wrong. The men are wearing helmets rather than the flat hats they brought with them, and the women cover their nakedness in cloaks before weaving had been invented.

They tamed the local wild life, Whippeticus Magnus, Ferretus Whiteleyus, Carthortiensis Legarius, Maximus Crappingus Cowicus and the Backwardus Flying Duckicus of Pudsey. They developed tools, particularly clubs for teaching the children and the wheel for bingo as well as that archetypal Yorkshire vehicle, the Sharrah, later perfected by that great Yorkshireman, Wallace Arnold, who first grasped the commercial opportunities of living in the only part of the world worth driving round. His Sharrahs gave lovely views outside and interesting opportunities for activity on the back seats.

The archetypal Yorkshire vehicle, the Sharrah, later perfected by that great Yorkshireman, Wallace Arnold.

Tykonian Man discovered the ancient Yorkshire technique known locally as Leg-ower, still vigorously practiced on both indoor and outdoor courts, particularly on Sunday afternoons. Which is why Sunday School was invented. Because of the wide-scale on which this was played, particularly in winter when there was no central heating, Tykonian Man multiplied and spread to the four corners of what was later to become the civilised world: the Tees, North Derbyshire, the Humber and the Pennines, which no one then had any reason for crossing since neither cricket nor rugby league, our ways of chastising the poor sods on the wet, westward side, had yet to be invented.

So they divided up into tribes each with its own Chief or "Gaffer", a Yorkshire title conferred out of respect. It could not be inherited for our ancestors, like us, were egalitarian accepting that Jack is as good as his master, and probably better. Centuries of selective breeding (and time passes quickly when you're having fun) allowed each tribe to grow in numbers and develop the characteristics best calculated to ensure survival.

The Mineworkus Tribe were bred small, cocky and stocky to survive underground. They moved into the south of Tykonia and began to dig big holes where they could get away from their wives, appearing above ground only at night which gave them the reputation of being extremely ugly. It was entirely justified. The Millworkus Tribe were deaf but could lip read, which later restricted the sale of CDs in Yorkshire. They gathered in the west and centre. At first they lived in the hills, or Attus Topus, to look down on every one, but gradually they began to move down to the valleys where the streams provided not baths - no Yorkshireman has been too keen on them - but water power for their machinery and sewage disposal for personal by-products, formerly left in great piles on the hills to feed birds, sheep and passing Lancastrians. In the valleys they built huge mills and lived round them, huddled back to back for warmth, it having been discovered by then that living front to front had too great an effect on the birth rate.

The Steelworkus Tribe lived mainly in Sheffield and Rotherham, though some developed the new art of Imperialism when they occupied Scunthorpe and raised the Yorkshire flag, and others moved north to Middlesbrough to huddle round fiery Northern furnaces to make useful instruments of birth control, such as swords knives and heavy hammers.

Thus Yorkshire became the cradle of a civilisation more important than the Euphrates, Sumaria or the Nile. Yet as long as the land bridge to Europe remained, not only would there be no work for bridge builders on Teeside, but it was possible for brutalised breeds from Germany, France or even the Urinals to come. So God decided, in the second of those interventions which demonstrate that he is a Yorkshireman, to sink the land between the Yorkshire coast and the Zuider Zee faster

The sea flooded in and landladies stood by all along the coast to repel boarders.

20

than the Coal Board could have managed after two hundred years of mining. The sea flooded in. Whitby, Scarborough, Filey, Bridlington and Hornsea became seaside resorts and three new tribes arose. The Fishworkus Tribe settled down the East Coast and began to catch the newly invented Cod and Haddock, leading to the development of fish and chip shops. The Dockworkus Tribe, the most striking of all, moved to Hull, Immingham and Grimsby to handle the export of sheep, sent as sex toys to Europe. Finally the Landladies Tribe stood by all along the coast to repel boarders. Yorkshire was complete. God was in his heaven above it, Tykonian Man was the master of the known universe.

As world population grew lesser breeds without the county began to eye this earthly paradise with envy. The threat of invasion increased and Romans were discerned in the gloaming. The famous Gastroroman, Julius Caesar, was lured by the world-wide reputation of Pie and Peas, Barnsley Black Puddens and that apogee of our edible arts, Yorkshire Pud. Archaeology can`t deal with anything that's been eaten so it was not realised until the recent discovery of a pottery price tag announcing Tykon Pud 2 Dinarius that Julius Caesar's prime object was to gain control of pud supplies.

He never got north of Kent. Perhaps it wasn't worthwhile at that time, the Batley Variety Club not being open and the Great North Road not yet started, though it was later funded by Rome as a Public Private Partnership. Roman money British slaves. So, it took two hundred years to complete. Caesar came and he saw, but didn`t conquer. He buggered off back home leaving the full invasion to 40 years later when a much bigger Roman army marched North, defeated the Tykonians, established their base at Catterick with R&R facilities in York and Spurn Point, named after the Roman problem of premature ejaculation. They had conquered as far up the East Coast as the Tweed or, to give it its Roman name, Lentheric, and up the west coast as far as Cockermouth, Roman translation Fellatio.

Yorkshire was now the centre of the known world, the Yorkshire Empire, sometimes misguidedly called the Roman Empire because Edward Gibbon came from the South and thought that sales in Rome might be better than Bradford. He never understood that York was both its capital and the birthplace of emperors, such as Severus, who set up his palace on a site now occupied by the Railway Institute, and the Emperor Constantime, the inventor of Greenwich Meantime, as well as the one-way chariot system in York in which some chariots were still stuck until they were towed out for the Park `n Ride Scheme. They have still not been claimed. Constantime ruled his empire from York with the help of a world-wide pigeon service organised from Barnsley where the birds were processed into pies to feed the troops on the Geordie Wall on return. He also developed a network of roads radiating out from York, so straight and efficient that Roman Chariots and Tykonian Sharrahs could reach Londonium faster than is now possible on the M1.Road works not yet having been invented.

Serious analysis of the Rise and Fall of the Yorkshire Empire must acknowledge that it was bound to fail. Yorkshire folk are neither natural imperialists nor interested in anything outside the county. Why bother to rule the world if you have to go away to do it? In Yorkshire every man is a King and every woman a Queen. So who could want to be Emperor? Yorkshire folk are naturally superior. Unlike the Southern English who began to believe themselves the world's ruling class once they found Yorkshire folk couldn`t be bothered. Southerners naturally want to go overseas because the south isn`t worth living in. So we gave up and the Empire and it went downhill faster than a sledge on Ingleborough. It`s historian, Taciturnus observed, "Sanguina Faultus nostra es".

Here at home, the former rulers of the world settled back on the beach at Scarborough with a good tablet of stone and the traditional Tyke response to crises overseas, "Couldn't give a bugger." Yorkshire remained as it was to be so many times afterwards, the last bastion of civilisation, sweetness and life.

The former rulers of the world settled back on the beach at Scarborough with a good tablet of stone.

It couldn't last, as Mother Shipton told her people, unfortunately retrospectively a thousand years later, and it didn't. Soon the waves of new invaders lured on by rumours of the sexual desirability of Yorkshire women and sheep, our gastronomic delights and our pure unsullied environment (for Teeside had not then been industrialised) came over the North Sea. First the Saxons, then the Angles all acute enough to recognise a nice place for a spot of murder, rape and pillage. Led by Hypotanuse, who knew all the angles but was something of a square (in comparison with the other two sides) and his son Obtuse, from whom Yorkshire folk inherit their bluntness, they spread throughout the land. The more acute angles headed for Calderdale, the more obtuse ones to the Don Valley where they found the women ready to try new Angles. To this day the places identified by the Cleckhecktonsedge Historical Association (C&IU affiliated) as Angular have been marked by signs planted along the roads to show whether they were settled by left or right angles.

The Angles and Saxons boosted our gene pool giving Yorkshire more striking tall blondes, both male and female, than a tanker of peroxide in London. They brought a new breed of lowland sheep which couldn't run as fast as theirs, making a valuable contribution to our diet and our dress, when it was discovered that wool could be spun and woven by women who hadn`t up to then had much to do. Except lie on their backs and think of Yorkshire.

Wool relieved unemployment among the Millworkus Tribe in the West Riding and gave names to a whole list of places hitherto blank on the map, such as Shipley, Shepley, Sheepscar and D'Ewesbury. People who had wanted to visit these places were now able to do so, increasing tourism in the Broad Acres building up the Sharrah industry. It also gave rise to a whole range of deeply unattractive jokes

When the Danes discovered how wonderful Yorkshire is, they decided to stay and contributed vocabulary.

about sex with sheep, the staple of Dales humour before television provided them with other things to do at night. The jokes, like the sheep, were later exported to Australia, which made Yorkshire wool buyers buy only New Zealand wool. They never know where the Australian had been.

No sooner had the Angles and Saxons intermingled their stock with the Tykonian Romans, (which is the prudish way the Yorkshire Genetics Eugenics and Spin Drying Association has of saying "had sexual intercourse with") when a far more terrifying wave of invaders appeared. The Vikings, led by the God Grim who gave his name to Grimsby and possibly also to Grimethorpe where the Chambers of Commerce directed the next thousand years to trying to get Grim's name changed retrospectively to "Happy", though in Grimethorpe Grim is a fairly exact description. The Vikings came in raiding parties now reinacted in outings to Meadow Hall, for a few days of murder, looting, rape and pillage, all codified by the venerable Bede and turned into the ancient Yorkshire sport of Rugby League. When the Danes discovered how wonderful Yorkshire is they decided to stay, adding yet another element to the genetic stock and a range of new place names, such as Royd, or clearing; beck, or stream; bugger, or sexual deviant; and butter, or sexual lubricant. Yorkshire became the pride of the Danelaw, a hard, tough world. The Wild North, as distinct from the soft South.

The Danes also contributed vocabulary: ligger down, Yorkshire's concession to sexual foreplay; addle a living, leading to the development of brass, an object of religious devotion; laiking to play as in Barnsley, Yorkshire's laike district; and bahn or going as in "ah'm bahn ter do summat", a statement of intent to pacify worriting (another Danish contribution) women but not necessarily acted on. Much of this remains current in Yorkshire, so true talking Tykes can make themselves understood in modern Denmark. When I went to support the "Nay" side in their Euro referendum I tried asking Scandinavian goddesses to ligger down a bit but quickly recovered from the wounds.

The next invaders were the Normans following Caesar's route via the South because it was softer. After giving King Harold one in the eye, they found that the North neither counted itself as English nor him as Gaffer. So to control those delicacies that had attracted him in the first place, the Pudsey Treacle Mines and the Sowerby Bridge Sorbet Mines, William the Conk had to fight Yorkshire all over again. Which he did by Norman or E.U. rules, laying waste and devastating the North. Which later became the standard regional policy applied by the South to the North by Henry VIII in the Pilgrimage of Grace in 1536, and Mrs. Thatcher. Who believed that phoenixes arise from ashes. So she turned the North into a heap of ashes as a favour.

The Normans contributed a few place names, "necessire" meaning shit house, and aristocratic family names: Fitzroy, Fitwilliam, Fitzherbert, Fitzthrowing and One Size Fitzall. Fitz means Lord or Bastard. They brought their own sport of Jus Primae Noctae. This quickly caught on as insatiable Yorkshire folk extended it into the second, third, fourth, fifth and every subsequent nocta, having more staying power than effeminate frogs. Having seen the potential of this sport, Yorkshire created a shrine for it where women folk had a special place. The scullery

The Normans were clearly afraid of Yorkshire, the Wild North, so castle building became a major local industry, employing thousands on public-private partnership contracts, on battlements, crenulations, draw bridges, and other splendid fortifications. This was building for keeps to protect our new lords from the loving admiration of their Yorkshire subjects. As a result, Yorkshire is the best castled, crenulated and embattled part of the country. Except for Wales which was similarly revolting.

The other Norman technique was to settle Yorkshire's wide open spaces not with ranches, but monasteries run by the Cistercians, Nosturcians, Francescans, Fish Friars and others of murkier habits, all recruited by advertising: "Go North Young Monk" "Get Closer to God" with "Convert the Tykes" danger money. Telling a Yorkshireman about God, the Good Life or Virtue is a waste of time.

The monasteries were established in the rolling acres of North Yorkshire from whence the people moved to the West Riding, going back only to rustle the sheep, deer, doves and pheasants the monks reared. The Tykes argued quite reasonably that if God wanted to convert them he surely wouldn't want to starve them first.

The Normans created the class system. Frogs on top as Lord this or Duke of that. Tykes were called villiens of various degrees of naughtiness. The hierarchy was: High Yorkshiremen, called Norman, Cedric, Cecil or Clarence, usually living in Harrogate or North Yorkshire and speaking a different language pronouncing "up" as "arp", as if the speaker had been chewing glass. Middle Yorkshiremen owned the mills, pubs, shops and fish shops. The Tykes, lived on chips and beer in terrace houses to cut down the heating bills with shared outside lavatories, also known as streets. Finally low Yorkshiremen, were known as serfs, the proletariat or shitkickers, all called Fred or Bert, their wife, or wives if they could get away with it, Gladys or Ethel.

The Great Yorkshire Story chronicles our rise to power by diligent hard work and careful attention to t'brass. Left alone to fend for usselves while monarchs plotted and empires rose and fell, Yorkshire got quietly on with mekkin a bob or two. We ensured the victory of Parliament (Good Guys) over the King (Proper Charlie) in the Civil War by locking the King out of Hull and denying him access to the newly developed Gannex lightweight armour supplied exclusively to Parliament. We gave neither support nor succour to the two Jacobite rebellions of 1715 and 1745, being neither romantics nor royalists and resenting drunken Scots trampling our lovely countryside.

We kept out of politics to get on with brass accumulation by our invention of the Industrial Revolution, and the first Yorkshire First Production. By developing machinery, driven by water then steam power, and concentrating production in "mills" with workers housed round about and dressed in shawls, flat hats and mufflers, Yorkshire made itself the richest part of Britain. Generating the wealth to build magnificient cities and support the idle, lay-about South. Yorkshire sheep worked double shifts to provide wool Yorkshire folk wore out their trousers quicker, from the inside, to keep the cloth pouring out and generate the wealth which allowed the Southern upper-classes to swan round the world and run an empire. Which kept them off our streets.

Thousands of workers lived in cities and mills, where Yorkshire literature flourished in dialect Almanacs aimed at "A daycent sooart if a Yorkshireman. Wun at's war nur sum, but not much". In the 1870s eighteen were published and the best of them, *The Clock,* became a vehicle for John Hartley, Yorkshire`s greatest poet who would have been Poet Laureate instead of Tennyson had Queen Victoria been able to understand a word he wrote.

This was Yorkshire's finest hour. It produced the Labour Party, a Yorkshire invention before the Scots took it up, our magnificent Town Halls, each a declaration of independence, the spread of allotments to replace the monasteries and the triumph of the "One Man One Shed" campaign.

Two centuries of growth, power, wealth and pride were brought to an end by the Southern ruling class. Having lost an empire, they began to screw Yorkshire, undermining our strength transforming us from a land of woollen mills to workhouses and Mrs Thatcher`s sado-masochist economics funding the job by closing mines, mills, steel plants, dockyards, engineering and chemical plants to make the Dole Office the most important building in Yorkshire towns. Yorkshire was drained, ditched, damned and changed from high-earning wealth generator to plaintive dependence because everyone in Yorkshire gets £1400 a head less in public spending per year than the Scots and seven hundred less than whinging Londoners who`ll probably spend it on drugs. We`d been buggered. Now it's time to get us own back. Yorksher Arise!

MEET THE FOLKS: A QUICK GUIDE FOR THE VISITOR

You can always tell a Yorkshireman. But not much. The true Tyke is tall, unless he's from the Mineworkus Tribe, in which case he's better described as stocky, overweight, unfashionable, because he doesn't give a bugger, and taciturn. He doesn't laugh much unless a Southerner chokes on his cocktail stick in front of him. He's well balanced, having a chip on each shoulder, and knows that the world is there to do him down. As well as his county. He's aggressive and can be extraordinarily bloody minded even if money isn't involved, which gives us the most amazing fights to the death as in the County Cricket Club, the N.U.M., the Labour Party and Illingworth Morris. The Fatwa (and again, we have the biggest and best) is a logical development of this Yorkshire propensity. We also generate the worst levels of road rage, parking place battles and missing teeth in the country. Yorkshire dentists would be the most profitable on earth. If Yorkshiremen paid their bills.

We have the lowest hygiene standards in the country, the fewest toilet rolls in toilets and the lowest propensity to wash our hands on leaving them.

He's not elegant and would think you were accusing him of sexual aberration if you said he was. He may smell a little and is known to pick his nose, even fart, though not very loudly, in company, particularly in lifts. Yorkshire women are much the same but wear skirts for identification. These days some wear trousers and in our cities on Friday nights, very little at all, though they conventionally dress as women or slop around in T-shirts and jeans with quick removal zips, even though many would look better in burkas.

Yorkshiremen shit more because they eat more and we have the lowest hygiene standards in the country, the fewest toilet rolls in toilets and the lowest propensity to wash our hands on leaving them. Why bother? It could be raining outside.
Yorkshire is a cocktail of awkward buggers that have come from everywhere and every race. A county with more words for daft, from barmpot to wossack, to pillock and limp under t`cap, than any other language isn`t exactly tolerant. Indeed, it's Yorkshire's job to tell folk what to do from playing cricket (hard) to treating women (ditto). Our wisdom is shared on a take-it-or-leave-it basis. We don`t care if our good advice isn`t taken. It`s everyone`s right to go to hell in a handcart and we know most other folk are daft. We don't make natural diplomats, so we usually tell them.

If truth be told (and we're the folk to tell it) Yorkshirefolk find few others pleasant, interesting or learnable from. Had we been monks we'd have been Trappists. Now we prefer canal banks and empty pubs to meditate in. The desire to be left alone is perfectly understandable in a county of awkward buggers surrounded by twerps. "Down t'coil oil weer t'muck slahts on t'winders" is a Yorkshireman's vision of heaven and rent free.

Yorkshire`s not a good place for women. They must be strident to get anywhere then they`re despised for being noisy. Far better to submit and recognise that a woman`s place was on her back in the scullery, or both. A child`s place isn`t being gently coaxed to self-expression but to shut up or be belted. Always for their own good. "Didn't do me any harm".

We`re unselfconscious. Our reactionaries are the stupidest, our wealth the noisiest, our red necks the rawest. Indeed, Yorkshire's not l00% civilised. Yet. *The Yorkshire Journal's* new. We've got more dog dirt and vomit in the streets though it does add colour and allows researchers to check the diet of the people without stomach pumps or watching them pig in. We beat wives (though only our own) more than most parts of the country. Our police kill more and relished their fights with the miners. Our football fans (particularly Leeds United) are the most thuggish, a propensity from which only Halifax Town is excused, not having any. We smell more than others individually and collectively, having more chemical plants, maggot farms and sewerage farms, indeed after ten unsuccessful years battling the smell from its

Copley plant, Yorkshire Water discovered that the residents quite liked it. Small wonder that our national Soap, Emmerdale, is filmed in a sewage farm at Esholt. We are, in short, basic.

When learning the language. Note that it varies. Dales dialect is incomprehensible in Barnsley. The East Riding is different again, particularly in vocabulary. First remove all traces of condescension, elocution, received pronunciation, lisps, and lah di dah. Harden your consonants and shorten your vowel sounds – "up" not "arp". Avoid the propensity of the Southern English to speak more loudly and slowly to foreigners. It carries the implication that the hearer is simple minded, and Yorkshire folk will resent that. Even those from Doncaster.

Yorkshire children are brought up on the principle of Oddinthinoise, Yorkshirefolk live by the rule of "If tha knows nowt, say nowt. If tha knows summat, say nowt." When approached they may not say anything at all. So exchange meaningful silences while staring into the middle distance in the hope that a flying saucer lands and gives rise to a brief conversation such as, "Oh look! Is that a Flying Saucer?" "`Appen".

Inscrutability and taciturnity are art forms in Yorkshire. When a Yorkshireman goes to a psychotherapist the therapist does the talking. The patient gives nowt away. The condition regularly diagnosed in America and Ireland as pseudologica fantastica, (or Archer Syndrome) is unknown in Yorkshire. People are not natural tellers of tall tales. Or any tales at all. Not worth saying owt unless it`s true. If we do you'd better believe it.

Sit next to your Yorkshireman and say something noncommittal like "Aye Up".

Spot your Yorkshireman. Start with males to invite less trouble - unless you speak like Julian Cleary, in which case you don't belong here. Recognise your prey because he looks unhappy as though the troubles of the world rested on his shoulders. They do. Sit next to him in Betty's Tea Room, Mrs Batty's Pudden Emporium, on the park bench, in Mother Hubbard's, or on the wall opposite the pie and pea stall. Don`t touch him or infringe his personal space, wider in Yorkshire than the South. Say something noncommittal, like "Aye Up". Don't stare or scrutinise. If well disposed he may say something philosophical. Such as "Na then, thee, `appen tha's not from these parts". That will be clear to him from your clothing and smell. Or he may merely say "Aaaayyy", as a kind of sigh of semi-acknowledgement. That`s is as close as you're going to get.

As a Tyke he's not well disposed to you but not ill-disposed either, even if you are a Southerner. Look suitably respectful and utter a few of those phrases used in old people`s homes to oil the wheels of conversation, such as "there's nowt so queer as folk". He`ll take that as an apology for your origins. Or "Ah'll go ter t'top of our stairs" though, being a Southerner, you may not have any. Say "Ah`m fair capped". No reply indicates he's limp under t'cap or dead. So you`ll have to begin again with another Yorkshireman. But a glimmer of response means Bingo! You're bridging Britain's greatest gulf between a true Tyke and the rest of the world. Even if he invites you to "tek thi'ook" (in which case don't look round for it. Just go) you've made a start. Now you can ger agate. Which doesn't mean take a gate home with you as a prize.

To build on that you need to talk Tyke. So first, a passionate appeal which springs from the heart.s

YORKSHIRE:
A LANGUAGE IN DANGER

Yorkshire is surrounded by enemies dedicated to destroying the Tyke tongue as a first step to undermining our national culture. To the North the Geordie nation speaks a form of pigeon Scots which they deliberately exaggerate to make themselves incomprehensible. Probably the most sensible thing for Geordies to do. To the West, Lancashire Hob Gobs are infiltrating their long vowel sounds and the propensity to pronounce an s as a z, into Todmorden where a Lancashire entrepreneur has taken control of the vital clog sole factory, making Yorkshire folk dependant on Lancashire clogs to clog dance any of them to death. To the South, or Subdoncastrium, we are better protected because accents remain defiantly Northern through Nottingham and Derbyshire. The Trent is the real boundary between the South, where consonants soften like brains and vowels posh up like peeresses, and the real world a.k.a. us.

There are also threats from within. Subversives from the ETU (Elocution Teachers Union} have been smuggled over the border disguised as old maids or BBC Producers to tell people that they'll never get on with an accent. In a few posh places like Harrogate, Yorkshire as she's spoken isn`t. The *Barnsley Chronicle* reports isolated cases of aspirates breathed from time to time as haspirates.

The death of Yorkshire industries killed by Southern bankers has eliminated a whole vocabulary of words such as "ee gies issen more airs n graces ner a deputy", "Ees as arrogant as an owerlooker" or "as ter been giing mi wife some bleach"? In textiles you could be "straight as a loith" or even "loith legged" or "as fast as a shuttle", while "t'wuzzers int'dye ouse no longer wuzz now t'BDA's cloised." What use is it calling about "t'dolly that stops t' loom when t'thread breaks", or about purn alignment piecen t'pieces together, or t'stang roller on t'loom, when all t'looms is gone. Or t'foddergang for feeding t'cattle when there's farm jobs only for machines and even t'lads that used to be told "tha's that lame under t'cap tha'll nobbut be a ploo lad" can`t get work plooin. In centrally heated homes it`s difficult to be "as black as t' fire back". Though kids still try.

Television gave rise to Yorkshire jokes like the Malton farmer who told Jonathan Aitken in his days as the first presenter of *Calendar* "tha wor like a rabbit stuck int'eadleets" or the nice old lady in the over sixty age range he mainly attracts who wrote to Richard Whiteley asking him to excuse her if he saw her watching in her nightie because *Calendar* wor well past her bed time and she wor staying up only for him.

Yet TV undermines Yorkshire. The media come from London and serve its interests, preferring South Eastern stories, blandised people without Yorkshire's hard edges, southern babble, not serious silence and received pronunciation in its fur coat and silk knickers, to real Yorkshire where knickers are optional.

Media bring us London fashions. Estuarial English (not the Humber estuary) as spoken by Tony Blair and other creeps desperate to show the common touch incomprehensible alternative comedy and the dreary, glum faced misery of East Enders

These crimes against the North go back to the days of the Rank Charm School and the chinless wonders of the Thirties when Yorkshirefolk were banned from the ether. Only in the war when the BBC found that it had to speak to real people, not talk down to them, did Wilfred Pickles, J.B. Priestley and Bill Holt begin to appear. By the Sixties a Yorkshire accent became that of the nation, a position it was pushed out of by the elocuted abominations of Ted Heath and Margaret Thatcher, and the takeover of the Labour Party by Public School Chaps.

The old discrimination, which held Herbert Clogworthy back from being Archbishop of Canterbury and Fred Gormley from being Warden of All Souls because both spoke broad Yorkshire, is back. So we must ensure that Yorkshire survives as a living language and gets its proper place as the tongue of the Tyke nation. Put Yorkshire on local radio stations instead of Pap. Have train announcements on GNER in Yorkshire as well as Urdu. Make those anonymous voices in lifts shout "Fust Floor - Gerrout If Tha`s Going." Make Yorkshire literature a compulsory part of the National Curriculum and the official language for all communications, from Central Government to the Yorkshire Region, and a recognised language in Europe`s. The Yorkshire language must be preserved and restored to primacy.The language in which God speaks can't be allowed to decline.

I visualise the day when a Hebden Bridge Garrison Keillor begins his tales from the Bridge, with "Nowt appened this week i'Ebden Bridge", or Calendar News comes in dialect: -
"Another fower pits closed i'South Yorkshire. Arthur Scargill said it showed as ow ee'd been reet all t'time an fowk should join t'Miners Union now it`s offering Co-op stamps", and "Yorkshire Watter announced as ow it 'ad lost another six million gallons o'watter. Following t'slahts ont'road ower ter Lancasheer. T'police said t'evidence ran out at a Dandellion an Burdock factory i'Rochdale." "Now sport. An' an 'Alifax Town lost agen. Poor Buggers. Fifty-eight ter nowt agin Pontefract Paraplygics. Thirteen fans were caught by t'police climbing t'fence. They wor med ter go back an' watch t'rest of t'game."

"Finally we're bahn live ower t't'United Nations General Assembly i'New York for t'speech ert' Yorkshire delegate, us plenipotentiary extra-ordinary Fred Murgatroyd KCGS (Knight Commander o't Golden Shuttle) Fred`s beeting t'rostrum wi 'is clog an' about to begin 'is speyk."

"Fred's beeting t'rostrum wi 'is clog an' about to begin 'is speyk."

Fred Murgatroyd:
"Order. Order, you buggers. Come on Giusbestovorder. Gius a chance lads. Let Yorkshire speyk.
(Order please gentlemen)
Mester Koffee Organic or whatever thi'name is ,an fellow delegates,ivverybody and me an all.
("Kofi Annan, fellow members, and the world.")
Ah`m bahn atta ave a call wit t`other
(I must meet urgently)
grate powers, America, Russia, on to Chinkies. I`Yorkshe we`re reet flummoxed
(with American and Russia and China. Yorkshire is worried -)

missen, ussens, thersens. Ah've allus thowt London guvanment couldn't
(all of us. I was sure the government in London)
organise a piss up in a brewery, they're that limp under t'cap
(was incapable)
but nah they've stuck their fillings inter Yorksher.
(but now they've interfered with our sovereign independence)
We can't reckon what they're laiking at, but they're bahn ter
(for no reason we can understand.)
pawse us int cods. Sitha they've got agate tekkin bits on Yorksher
(They'll do us harm. They've taken bits of Yorkshire)
ter gie em ter Lancashire an Durham. They've sammed Barlick
(into Lancashire and Durham. They've taken Barnoldswick)
ant'fells to hugger em off, chip'oils, pay'oils, cloises an
(and carried it off lock, stock and)
fowk an all. They've took us jobs, us brass, us Ridings an us Councils
*(barrel. They have weakened us economically and abolished our Ridings and
County Councils).*
It's fair for us capped. Ah sez ter t'barmpots I
(We are puzzled. I tell Her Majesty's Government that)
London we're nivver barn ter tek it liggen dahn. If it cums ter
(we object. If it reaches)
fratching we're not flayed. We'll a them clumping gormless set
(conflict we have no fear. Her Majesty's Government)
pots knackered I no time afore we giup. So Gerrof. An Gerrome.
(will meet with strong resistance in its declared intention. Desist.)
An ah war telled t'get thi ter gi' us us seat on t'Security Council.
(my people demand their independence and recognition by the U.N.)
Theer int any turd way I'this. It's gie us or gerrome."
(There is no alternative. Concede to us or leave the building).

(Wild applause from Russian delegate. All others join in singing Ilka Moor Baht Blair).

Roll on Home Rule for Yorkshire with Yorkshire language compulsory in schools and
our means of communication with the world and ussens. If tha wants to play a part
and be ready to share our triumph, get on with learning us language. It's speyken
by more fowk than Gaelic or Welsh. It has its own grammar, vocabulary and
literature. With the help of this Shorter Yorksher Primer tha'll be able to teach thissen
Tyke within a few days. Just follow the text, soak your tonsils in Tetleys and you'll be
able to make yourself understood at the Grimethorpe Sports and Social, enjoy the
ambience of the Kellingley Miners Welfare, get served at Mother 'Ubbards and even
go into local hostelries without being beaten up before you can get a drink. Add a
flat 'at, a muffler, sew up your pockets and you may even pass for a native. The
highest form of recognition Yorkshire can confer. So, let's go wi Yorksher.

STEP ONE: SITHA AND SAYTHA

FOR YORKSHIRE FIVE YEAR OLDS (AND SOUTHERNERS OF ALL AGES)

First you need a basic grammar and yammer to help you tell Tyke talk from Southern mutter. Teach Thissden Tyke in seven days. Then tha can join t'lads. Reet. Let`s Gerronwiit. The best way to stawrt speykin reet is to begin (gerrin) wi't'kids int'schools or scoils.

Take Barnsley where primary scoil children begin Yorksher with the very latest teaching methods. The Subdoncastrians learn English by looking and saying with Janet and John and French by following the adventures of the famille Deranged or Desgranges or whatever. T`Barnsley Association of Yorksher Taychers (Meetings Monday 8.30 at the New Lodge Hotel) has opted for Sitha and Seytha with the Blenkinsop Family. Take a typical page:

Sitha our Enoch.
Sitha our Ethel.
Sitha us Councilouse.
Sitha us Wippet. It`s peed ont floor agin.
Wots up wiem saytha.
They look like a week on neets.
Our Enoch`s just thumped our Ethel int breadbasket. Int ee a norty lad.
Nivver mind. Us Dad`ll thump is lug. Thump is lug dad. Thump is lug.
Sitha us Mam.
Sitha us Dad.
Us Mum`s bawling agen.
Wot`s us mum bawling for nah saytha?
She`s belling er ead off cos she war as throng as Throp`s wife wen she
  Anged ersen wit` dishclout when us Dad cum ome kalied agen.
Us Dad`s reet sloshed.
Us Dad`s been downt`boozer all day an spent all us brass. An it int dole day
  til Thursday.
Mam`ll belt is ead in.
Belt is ead in Mam.
Belt is ead in.
Na t`t`tally man`s cum for t`telly.
Int it grand i' Barnsley. Eee it is. Int it.
Like nowt on t'earth.
Oh aye it is.

A Nexercise

Now answer these questions sitha:
Wot has Enoch done to Ethel?
Wot as Dad dun wit brass?
Wot day duz Dad sign on?
Az mam wun at Bingo?
Ow much is a cake an' chips?

If you can't answer these questions you are limp under t`cap and educationally underprivileged. Watch out or you`ll end up at Giggleswick or Woodhouse Grove Instant Public Schools.

On t`other `and, them as lerns ter speyk reet can get down t`mines, werk as tatters, or go int`t`black pudden an clog factories, an mek a bob or two an sup therrsens stupid an ave a reet grand time. So stop readen` t`book ere if yer`ve answered reet an' fork out another five bob for us book on *Advanced Tyke Talking*. Sing t`Barnsla Anthem an' ave another pint.

Now study various examples of Tyke expression prior to further tongue-twisting to savour the beauties of the Yorksher thought-process.

Drunk as a Fiddler`s Bitch: If quadruple Co-op stamps were given for the purchase of four or more gallons of beer he would have done well to take a suitcase to the hostelry with him.

Eez peed ont chips: He has frustrated our plans. See Magaret Thatcher`s comment on President Reagan`s decision to bomb Libya and Bradford (where no-one noticed but damage estimated at 17p was sustained).

Strong as Chip Oil Vinegar: He has not taken the Charles Atlas course.

As Mucky as a Sink Oil Tooad: He will never grow rich on the Divi from the purchase of a Co-op carbolic.

If ee fell oft Co-op eed fall int Divi Ole: He is a rather fortunate person. Usually applies to building workers, anyone outside the textile industry and to self employed Black Pudding Blenders.

Snap: Miner`s lunch, food. When tae roof is very low miners say "t`seems that low tha mun tek pancakes for thi snap."

Ee wudn`t part wit reek ov is own muck: Not the most generous of men.

Oil: This can be poured on almost any troubled noun as in coil, oil, chip oil, lug oil, cake oil, bobby oil, pit oil, or even used with its own adjectives as in mucky oil. More complex uses: Ass oil – grate under fire place. Pay oil – Pea and Pie Shop. Slap oil – puddle. Delf oil – quarry. Bug oil – cinema like t`Pavilion i`Shipley where t`Commissionaire used ter say "Don`t spit int ashtrays. Ah wants t`tab ends." But it`s so long since t`Pavilion closed that yer can see t`films it used ter show on TV now. In the rest of the country the word oil has been taken over by Esso. Correct Yorkshire usage is best explained by drilling expert Arthur Blenkinsop who rose from being Under Deputy at Wombwell Main to the Most Boring Official of the N.C.B. Yorkshire Region. On a lecture tour of America, Blenkinsop was asked by one smartalec: "If holes were oils what was the stuff that came out of them?" "Grease yer daft buggar" was Blenkinsop`s witty reply.

Sodjer: Means soldier if applied to someone in uniform. If applied to someone out of uniform it can be assumed not to be a compliment.

You are now ready to proceed further into the mysteries of the Tyke tongue so get yer glottalsops ready an GETSTUCKINLAD.

GETTING THISSEN FIT

LANGUAGE reflects character. This is a hard county breeding hard folk who speak hard sounds. Yorksher is more wearing on the mouth than any other Lingua Franca. Ask Frank. So we talk less. When Tykonian Man arrived in the Bird Eyes Age among the first sounds he uttered "g-g-g-g" figured prominantly. The hard G has remained with us ever since. Consonants are the landmarks of language and must be given prominence and tret hard. Like shunting engines conveying one batch of minor sounds to or from another.

Southerners pronounce G with the front of the mouth. We use the back which must be specially reinforced by taking a West Riding County Council road sweeper`s brush that`s seen good service down Carr Lane, dipping it in best creosote, igniting and then brushing the back of the mouth and the tonsils vigorously. Take the brush out and you`ll be pronouncing the Yorkshire G-g-g. The reinforcement will also allow the mouth to tolerate the Cleckheaton K-k-k. These are sounds for men which reveal any imperfections in the rib cage.

The Tyke T`t`t is even more vital, being used instead of the English word "the". To acquire this in quick time: prepare a strong Madras curry sauce, stir in half an ounce of black peppers, eighteen chillies, a quarter pound of cayenne pepper and six pounds of Colman`s mustard. Heat on North Sea Gas to ensure a bang and put your tongue into the boiling liquid. It can also be used for cauterising boots. The pain can be eased by blowing cold air over the tongue tip while tapping it rapidly against the cool roof of the mouth. As the screams die down you`ll be making the Tyke T`t`t. You may also be drowning this book in spray. Carry on until you can make the sound without passing water as in "take the horse to the wooden building" which becomes TEKTOSSTUTUT.

Prepare a strong Madras curry sauce and put your tongue into the boiling liquid.

38

Tykonomy

SPEYK teachers in pubs all over the county will tell you that the other key to proper speyking is ECONOMY. This is also part of our character. A bloke in Barnsley tried to compete with the supermarkets by offering an immediate money back guarantee at his grocery. One morning he was amazed when a little kid came to get his mum`s money back on two toilet rolls. The explanation was quite simple: "Company didn`t come".

We`re as cautious with language as with brass. One is chucked around like a man with no arms, the other like Herbert Long who had no tongue.

These are the basic rules of Tykonomy in speyking:

1. The ideal is total silence: Ear all see all say nowt.

Some of us attain this ideal and never have to buy another round for the rest of our lives. This is known as ODDINTHINOISE or SHUTINTHICAKEOIL. All Yorkshire children take compulsory lessons in these subjects.

2. Where speech is essential a multi-purpose word which can mean whatever the hearer likes it to mean can often be used.

Southerner: *"Does this road lead to Pickeringdale Pike?"*
Articulate Dalesman *"Appen".*
Southerner: *"Thank you my good man".*

`Appen it doesn't, but then it`s fun finding out. Other useful variations of the Mixendon Multinoise are "By Gum" which can be inserted into conversations at hourly intervals to show you are awake and interested, or "Eck" a contraction of the Latin Ecce Homo, the pet name of Ben Dover the Yorksher Oscar Wilde.

3. Never use a whole word where it can be contracted. "Something" takes 1.85 seconds to say, "summat" 0.94 seconds. Anything and nothing can be contracted to owt and nowt, a process which gives commercial travellers from the Rosencratz Clothing and General Supply Co. in Leeds the fastest turnaround in the country. Their conversations with shopkeepers run as follows:

"Owt?"
"Nowt".
"Tarra".

4. Where words are known to both parties in a conversation they can be dropped altogether except for some symbolic noise. Take the following early morning conversation in millions of Yorksher homes as the wife strives to get hubby down for breakfast. The old shout of "Clogs is going past" having received the traditional reply of "Put mine out and see if they`ll go", the conversation carries on as follows:

Mam: *"Y`up?"*
Dad: *"ibed"*.
Mam: *"Grup"*.
Dad: *"Shrup"*.
Mam: *"Grup"*.
Dad: *"Mup"*.

Us Mam and Dad can then return to the higher reaches of humour. Mam sez "It int fit ter put a dog out. Don`t forget thi snap". If you live in Rotherham you`ll be woken up by the sound of the sparrows, coughing. Other candidates for emasculation are "will" or "have to". "Next bus`ll be late tha`ll atta run". By the same token "the" should be used only when talking to royalty or the manager of the Devonshire Arms at Grassington. It`s not generally known that economising on "the" during the twenty third and twenty fourth Yorkshire Wars (also known as First and Second World Wars) we saved so much newsprint in Yorkshire that it was vital in winning the war. For its efforts the county was awarded the George Cross so we can be referred to as the Kings Cross County. "T" can of course be confusing to Southerners. A visitor to Bradford told the newspaper lad he couldn`t remember which paper he`d preferred on his last visit but it had begun with a `t`. The lad replied scornfully "That dun`t `elp. There`s t`Telegraph, t`Argus and t`Observer".

5. Make as many things as possible singular so you can replace "re" by the "Sedburgh zis" as in "Picture zis loosing". The soldiers are marching becomes "sodger zis marching". The only exception to singularity is talking about yourself. Yorkshiremen are entitled to use the royal "we", though all except Jimmy Saville have let Lady (Muck) Thatcher use it too. We still refer to ussens as us as in "Usmam" and "Usdad" or "gie us one".

6. The haspirate is `ateful and an `eadache, to be used only when chatting to the Hearl of `Arewood over `is wall. The former editor of the *Pudsey Examiner* could only have been a Tyke. As the season for the ducks to migrate backwards to Stanningley approached he would leap round the office hitting the staff on the head and bawling "I`m t`eaditter".

A Nexercise

You can now learn rules four, five and six by repeating four hundred times the battle cry of the `Avercake Lads. "T`officerzis `itting t`osses ower`t`ead wi`t`whips. T`officerzis `itting t`osses ower t`ead wi t`whips".

7. Vowel sounds must be short and sharp. Don`t ooo and aaarse around like a Young Conservative at an haunt bawl. Southerners swill vowel sounds round the gob as if savouring a fine wine "aaay saaay ooold maaan". We spit them out which is why no one up here can sing "Kaahmen to the Garden Maud" properly. Remember:

Aaaah - a as in knackered
Uuuuh - u as in cum
Eye   - I as in din
Ooooh - o as in `og

These short, sharp noises are best produced after eating half a dozen Barnsley Black Puddings each immersed in half a pound of best mushy peas. This mixture will produce a generous supply of short sharp rushes of air, the basic raw material for good vowel sounds. Since you will be speaking from the soul it is advisable to wear Y Front underwear when practising your Yorkshire vowel sounds.

A Nexercise

Repeat the following 80 times in Yorksher, "If there were another war this war will be worse than t'last war war war" it translates as "If there war another war this war`ll be war n`t`last war".

8. The final principle of economy is to merge words together. On the Bricklayer principle, examine your words. Do they look compatible? Bang them together in your mouth. Do they merge easily? Will knocking a bit off help? Where "give me" is ugly and unattractive "gimme" has a nice flow to it. So does the advanced student`s "gius". Hard edges can be softened. The main techniques are:

(a) "have not" can be softened into "mp" as in "Iampgorrit" (I have not got the object to which you are referring).

(b) F can either be left off or softened to v, a technique first perfected by the early Methodists. Tired of hostile crowd reactions in the pit villages, they agreed to the crowd`s plea by leaving the f off. A request for matches, pipe, tobacco, or, in Batley, money, can be simplified to ASANYONYERANYONYER (has any of you gentlemen a small amount of the object in question on your person).

(c) T has done well enough out of us at the beginning of words so it can be softened at the end. Elementary students should turn it into an r. "Would you kindly remove yourself" becomes "gerroff", the courting cry of the Yorkshire mill lass. The officiating archpriest, the Con. Sec. completes this with the traditional response: "shurrup". More advanced students use the Glasshaughton glottal stop to complete the "t word" with a silent "Glug".

Translation

Translate the following into English. Three marks for a fully correct answer, two if one word is wrong, one for a partially right answer. None for a baffled gurgle.

Standard Yorksher

Standard English

1.PUTWOODINTOIL — Kindly close the door
2.INTITORFUL — Isn`t it rather awful
3.THADBERRERLERRERGERITERSEN — It is perhaps advisable to allow her to make her own choice
4.YERNIVVERMISSASLICEOFFERCUTCAKE — I`m sure your husband wouldn`t mind
5.ASTERGOROWTTERGUIS — Have you anything to give us?
6.SUMMATSUPEER — Something would appear to be wrong here
7.GERRITETTEN — Please hurry up and eat your food
8.WASAMARRERWIIM — What, I wonder, could possibly be the matter with that gentleman?
9.IAMPGORRITWIME — I have not in fact got the object to which you are referring
10.ISEEGOINGOME — Is he about to set off for home?
11.ASTERGORRITWITHEE — Have you got the object to which I am referring with you?
12.AYAMFTEERDNOWT — I have not actually heard anything
13.EESEZITINTISBURRABERRITIZ — He says that the object is not in fact his but I think that it is
14.EELAFTERGIEOWWER — He will have to desist
15.OURLASSEZGORRABUNINTOVEN — My sister appears to have conceived
16.ATELLTIMBURREEWUDDENTLISSEN — I did in fact tell him but he was reluctant to listen

Astergorritreit?   Thenthamungerritlernt.   Ahclowtthiifthaduntgerronwiit.

With 48 marks thasdunreetwell. Getthipuddinetten. 35-47 tha`ll do but tha`ll atta spend a few neets on refresher course in any C.I.U. affiliated College of Father Education. Between 20 and 34 marks you`re either trying to live down a Grammar School education or low origins somewhere just south of Doncaster.

Between 10 and 19. Go to Castleford, move directly to Castleford..
Do not collect benefit.

**Below 10. You`re hopeless.** Either a Public School man or a member of Her Majesty`s Government. In the words of that witty reply, much favoured by graduates of the Grimethorpe College of Wit and Repartee, "get knotted."or something anatomically more challenging

More Vocabulary

Bob: Until the intervention of the Decimal Currency Board this had two meanings. "if tha Bob dunt gie our Bob t`bob `at tha Bob owes our Bob our Bob`ll gie tha Bob a bob ont`nose."

Jock: Food, lunch, sandwiches. Up in Slowitt (or Slaithwaite if yer believe t`atlas) they`re that daft they run t`watter an t`gas up t`same pipe. A process YE has now improved on by including the electric too.

A farmlad more slow-witted than most dropped his jacket into the midden. Farmer arrived to find him poking round in the manure with a big stick trying to find it. "Nay" sez the farmer "it`s no use getting thi jacket out of there, it`ll reek to high heaven". "Aye" said the lad "but mi jock`s int`pocket".

"It's no use gettin' thi jacket out o' there, it'll reek to high heaven!"

Ither: Either. Ask anyone in the Wallace Arnold Sports and Social Club at Royston whether it`s Ither or Either. They`ll tell you "awther`ll do".

Baht: Not only applied to `ats on Ilkla Moor. In the 23rd Yorkshire (or First World) War a Yorkshire lad enrolled in a Somerset regiment. Asked why he was on parade without a rifle he replied "ee nivver gie us ony on em". Asked for explanation he could only say "I ant got none". This reduced the whole regiment to baffled incomprehension. At great expense an interpreter was fetched down from civilisation (actually Dodworth). After conversation with the rifleless Tyke he reported to the C.O. "Well what does he mean then?" bawled the Commander. "Ee sez ees baht" said the interpreter. *When t`lads say they`re "supping baht" it`s your round.*

43

Agate: To start, get on with. When our American allies were helping in the 24th Yorkshire (or the Second World) War, by keeping our girls happy while Yorkshire lads fought the Hun, one took a Shipley lass up the Glen. "Gee honey, how about a kiss and a cuddle" he breathed passionately. "Well get agate then" she replied. When he came back with one, she`d gone off to t`Rosse for a Babycham.

Sitha: No relation to Anton Karas or the Harry Lime theme, this is a multi purpose word fulfilling much the same role as the "Now Hear This" announcement in the American Navy. Frowned on by middle class parents in Brighouse where they`re that daft they put t`pig ont wall ter watch t`band go by. The Jarrat family were going up in the world. Little Richard said to his dad as they walked down Bonegate "Sitha yon bloody dog ont job." Dad replied "How many bloody times have I to tell you not to say sitha".

Allus: As in the refrain of the famous song "I`ll be luving you, allus".

Neet: As in "Ah`ve just supped a bottle o`hisky". "Good heavens, was it neet". "Wor it eck. It wor broad dayleet".

Lame under t`cap: He is not the most intelligent of mortals. Can also be applied by people in Cleckheaton to the inhabitants of Spenborough and by those in Spenborough to denizens of Cleckheaton.

Laike: In Barnsley they`ll tell you of the fish and chip shop on the New Lodge Estate where the locals all hang around on Monday, skint because the investment of their redundancy pay with William Hill has inexplicably failed to prosper. A large Rolls Royce pulls up and an upper class voice asks "Is this the way to the Lake District?" All reply with one voice, "You`re there. Everybody laikes on Monday". The Castleford variation is the kid`s essay on "The Great Lakes" which covers Cricket, Soccer and Rugby League. To laike is to play, from the old German lacken: drawing dole money. Ask any o`t` lads at Hoyland why he only works three days a week and he`ll tell you "Cos ah can`t manage if ah laikes fer more ner two".

Nessy: Derived from the Scandinavian Nesscheisserhausen or meeting place, a place where motions are passed. Corrupted into lavatory. In the Dales where the old fashioned thunder box is still found the Appletreewick Truant Catcher and Rodent Operative called on Mrs. Robinson to reprimand her because young George hadn`t been to school for six weeks. When he concluded with the warning that if this went on he would have "to take the necessary steps" she was unconcerned. "Then us`ll atta do us business int`field".

AS AN OUTWARD BOUND COURSE

For two German parachutists who dropped on Barnsley during the war talking Tyke was a crash course.   From an elite SS Unit their task was to undermine British morale by sabotaging the Barnsley Black Pudden Factories then working overtime to keep up Black Pudden Supplies to the Far and Middle East. As they disguised themselves as natives, rubbing coal dust on to their faces, whippet pee into their boots, two Barnsla lads passed talking about a lass.

"Oo war shi wi?"
"She war wi'ersen".
"Oh. Washee?"
"She war .Quit worriting".
"Mein Got in der himmel" said the Germans as they gave themselves up. "They've dropped us in China".

Had they had this book to learn the language their experience could have been so different and Germany may even have won the war, not against Yorkshire, of course, but possibly against the softer South.   A similar sad fate attended on Clarence Fitzthrowing Smyth (Eton, Christs's and the Garrick) when he arrived at Leeds Station on his way to shoot at Bolton Abbey - well not the building, of course, the birds. And not our kind of birds but the aristocracy's kind. Clarence hailed a porter:-

Porter: Weer ta bahn me old luv?"
Clarence: Don't be impertinent my good man. I don't love you. I'm a married
              man and I wouldn't dream of staying in a barn. Where's the Queen's
              Hotel?
Porter: Appen. Tha looks like t`Queen's reight for thee.
Clarence.   (by way of police conversation) What a crowd. What's happening?
Porter: Football's loosin.
Clarence: Oh I'm sorry to hear that. I thought Leeds would win.
Porter: Nah yer great gawpead they've not lost they've won – match's loosin.
              No point in standing ont terraces warching t`daisies grow.
Clarence: Is there a train back to London immediately?

The bright pupil will of course know that "Church's loosin" does not necessarily mean God Nil, Atheists 6. To avoid misapprehensions like this you will need to master the Tyke tongue.

Clarence, unfortunately, didn't though he did attempt to make what he hoped would be a more physical contact with some of the attractive Tykesses he glimpsed in Bradford. Asking where he could discover more of the breed he was directed to the Idle Working Men's Club (the name of the part of Bradford not a description of the disposition of the people, though most of them are born idle). There he presented himself at the door to be greeted by what he instinctively recognised as a tribal elder. The Sec hockled on Clarence's boots and speyk thus:-

Doorman: Are yer t`turn?
Clarence: I beg your pardon?
Doorman: Are yer t`artist?
Clarence: Oh are you having some kind of exhibition?
Doorman: Wot club yer from?
Clarence: Oh Clahbs. Well…the Athenaeum and Whites.
Doorman: Nivver eard on em. Are they filleted?
Clarence: I beg…
Doorman: Well oo`s t`Con.Sec.?
Clarence: Well…Norfolk…
Doorman: Eddie Norfolk! You old beggar fr Lower Wortley. Any pal on Eddie`s Is a pal o mine. Gerrin wi yer.

Inside, Clarence's lug oils will be assaulted by an electronic organ belting out (S)ailing. He`ll need wellies to wade through the spilt ale, but he can`t fail to be impressed by the Chargey Dafairs, the Con. Sec. sitting in state in his box and occasionally bawling "GIUSBESTOVORDER". This translates roughly as "please be quiet". He might even address himself to Clarence, as he edges nervously across the room. "Wots tha mean tha great gobslotch moochin round while Arry`s obliging ont`organ. Park thiseen an give t`poor sod a chance. Ee`s doin is best. Thee sidahn an belt up".

This does not mean "prepare for take off" unless Clarence has stumbled into the Sunday lunchtime strip and nature study.

Con. Secs. can even change the names of persons and groups. One neet at the Askerne Antediluvian and Clog Puddlers` Institute a rock and roll group arrived, all long hair and million megawatt amplifiers. "What`s thi name?" said the Con. Sec. "Anderson`s Apocalypse" they replied. "Tha`s t`Four D`s toneet" he said chalking "FOWER DEES" on his blackboard.

Having found a seat, Clarence is approached by an enormous giant of a man who addresses him "Wotyergonneravluv?" Ignore the endearments. This is not a sexual advance and should be answered with "Giusagilloets" or if Clarence wants to make friends, "Letsavajarallround". Clarence shouldn`t be shocked if one of his new mates says to the waiter "Gie us a touch luv". He wants a dash of lemonade. The drink will have brought new friends for Clarence. At first he should merely listen to what they have to say while throwing in an occasional "ByEck", "Bloody Ummer" or even "Wellallgotertopovourstairs".

As his confidence grows Clarence can even use a pause in the flow to try a phrase such as "Owerthebuggersgerrinonthen". In Bradford where excitement still lingers over City`s recent (1911) F.A. Cup victory this will produce a discussion on football. In Castleford it will be taken as a reference to Cass. In the summer it will lead to an analysis of God`s perversity in not giving Yorkshire "BESTOVORDER" in the weather, though possibly with an admission that he can`t favour his own side too much. It may even be understood as a reference to how the Brass Band Championships have been rigged against Grimethorpe (again). Whatever the subject Clarence has begun a conversation.

He should merely listen to what they have to say while throwing in an occasional "By Eck" or "Bloody Ummer".

When it ends he can immediately trigger off another and draw attention to the fact that it`s someone else`s round by quietly smacking his lips and murmuring "Notabadjarovaleere. Damnsiteberretnertpissahadtotherneet". Recollection and discussion will pour forth. With a bit of luck he might even get a long argument on the exact difference between London beer and lemonade. As now Clarence will be thoroughly accepted. Before he even needs to speak again the room will suddenly fill with the Con. Sec`s voice interrupting Marion Golightly`s rendering of "Velia oh Velia my witch of the wood" with the shout of "Cumonlads. Givtpoorcow a chance -Oh `ang on. Ah see t`pies av cum. Yes it`s mate an taty fifty pee , steak an kidney a quid. Yes lads t`pies av cum". No more need be said. The rest of the evening is ATENSWILLTIME until the steward wishes them all "God Speed and sleep tight" with a friendly "Cumonlads. Seeyerdrinksoffnah". Clarence as dun reet well which should be some consolation for what`s going to happen to his ring of confidence when he goes home.

Now some more lessons so GERAGATEANGERRONWIIT.

NOBBUT A BIT MORE

Vowel sounds are short and sharp but not when vowels follow each other. Then employ the Drighlington dypthon. "After Dad`s death I was going home down the road past the school when I saw a ghost round a post" would be translated "Atta Dad`s deeath I war bahn hooam down t`road past t`scooil when I saw a ghoooast goin raaand a pooast." Right? Well do it again. (This in fact refers to the Stanningley ghooast which war hobbut a pooost). Where two vowels come together don`t blur them, pronounce both separately as in me-at, se-at, fo-am. The long I becomes ee as in seet (sight) a pronunciation which has caused a lot of doctors to make patients take their trousers down when all they needed was optical treatment. But if it`s an ight as in feyt it isn`t a garden party or something worse than death, but a bloody set to. Also O on its own when it can`t be shortened to a cry of pain becomes owa as in the Conservative Party also known as the Towaries who have always been a minority in Yorkshire since they lost office in the disputed election of I487 after misguidedly supporting the Lancastrians in the War of the Roses.

You is a sound very rarely heard in Yorkshire. Being more friendly we prefer thou, tha or in emergencies t` as in "Weer ta bahn lass" or "Where are you going to, my pretty maid". In moments of extreme anger Ossett Fish-puddlers have been known to resent "thou" and reply "Don`t thee thou me thee thou thissen and see how tha likes thee thouing" but this is rare. Normally it`s "you" that is regarded with suspicion because it looks like part of an income tax demand or some official pronunciation. The only real problem is that with sloppy pronunciation it can be mistaken for other words. Opera North were playing at the Heckmondwike Promenade concerts during the strike by the Cleckheaton Federation of Sewage and Related Trade Operatives. "Weer`s t`arpist?" demands the Conductor scanning the ranks only to have the fifth violinist bawl back "Behind t`piano, weers tha?" This same orchestra would never play Greig having been ordered not to pee agin t'suite in the interests of decorum.

Careful speyk training can eliminate this problem. In Sheffield up t`Wicker weer t`watter runs ower t`weir, they prefer dou to thou so greet people here with "Now den dee wot da doin wi di sen".

Finally there are various conjugations which can only be learnt by heart.

1. To bi (verb), as in Shakespeare`s "to bi or not to bi". It conjugates Am, Thart, Eez, Sheez, Usiz, Yar, Themis. The negative is usually obtained by putting not at the end. "I arent, tharnt, eeint, sheeint etc". Elocution teachers have worked hard to stamp out this usage. At South View Juniors, Yeadon, the teacher was taking names for the

school trip, when Jack Riley loudly announced "I aren`t going". He was hauled out as an example. "Jack you know it should be `I am not going, you are not going, he is not going, she is not going, we are not going, they are not going`". Jack was unimpressed. "Int no one goin then is there" he announced. Jack should have been doing the teaching. "Ah sharn`t an ah weyn`t say owt but I aren`t" is reet Yorksher.

2. The future of to bi is willa, witta, willee, willer, willus, willyer, willem.

3. To gi (verb) conjugates gimme, githee, giim, gier, gius, giem, giiower, giup, usually followed by gerroff.

4. Some verbs cause problems only in the past tense. Put becomes putter, though the class sneak in our primary school made a fool of himself when he told teacher "Miss, Austin`s putten `putten` when ee shud ave putten `put`".

5. Missen. Visitors often assume that Mr. Missen is either Yorkshire`s gaffer or its most popular personality, having misheard our toast as we raise us Dandelion and Burdock "here`s to me and my wife`s husband not forgetting missen". He is naturally more popular than Mr. Thissen who doesn't get owt for nowt. Missen was immortalised in the 24th Yorkshire War when Brian Dean, a pilot from Pudsey who used to fly his bomber backwards, was listing his crew as safe after returning from bombing the Obergurgle Saurkraut Factory. "There`s Smith the Bombadier, Blenkinsop the Navigator, Fotheringay-Smythe the lavatory cleaner who put in meritorious service over Germany with the biggest drop, and lastly there's Missen" he reported, thus giving rise to the famous phrase "One of our pilots is Missen". It conjugates Missen, thissen, hissen, erssen, ussens, yersenns, thessens. Repeat this forty times until you get the sense of it. By the way if you include brussen you`ll get stuffed.

Talking Tyke by Numbers

Tha`s now ready to speyken thee Yorksher (or Lethigobflap). For this you need to know what to say. Stick to what`s safe. Emergency wards all over the county are choked with would be linguists having bottles removed after trying concepts too advanced for their ability. So here`s a guide to speyking by numbers which will allow you to make one thousand do-it-yersen Yorksher sentences. All have been tried and tested in the Batley Variety Club, Walton British Legion and the Coal Board office at Allerton-by-Water before it was turned into a drive in brothel. Just pick any number with three figures, say 147 for the number of honest folk in London. Take the first phrase in column one, the fourth in two and the seventh phrase in column three and combine them to make:

"Hellsbells an buckets o`blood but t`aint true as work killed no one cos even osses turn ther arses to it don't yer reckon". Bingo. This will (a) identify you as a true Tyke talker and (b) get a conversation going with whatever natives you care to address it to and (c) commit you to nothing at all. It is therefore very useful for third way (the "h"is silent) political speeches. Alternatively take 271 as the average I.Q. of Yorkshiremen. Go on try it. You`ll soon have more sayings than Sheffield has Sithas or London has loonies:

Column Wun	Column Two	Column Three
1. Ell`s bells an buckets o`blood	1. Tha munt ever be t`main man at a weddin or a funeral	1. But, ahm not ter worry ower much
2. Sitha	2. There`s nowt so queer as fowk	2. Tha knows
3. It`s fair cappin but	3. Yer nivver know oo yer friends are	3. Ah reckon
4. By Ummer but	4. T`int true as work killed no one cos even `osses turn their arses to it	4. When all said an done
5. If there`s one thing I say	5. Ah`m nobbut fair ter middlin	5. Any on yer can tell
6. It`s past t`time someone said	6. It`s thronging wi folk int`snicket	6. Still t`truth nivver urt any-one
7. By Gum	7. Ale weant work an it weant laike quietly awther	7. Don't yer reckon
8. Thas got ter admit as ow	8. Possers an set pots 'll nivver cum back ageean	8. Anyone wi`t use of is een can see.
9. Ah must say	9. Chuckin out time int boozers int reet	9. Wouldn`t ta say

These should last you for years of illuminating conversation over dominos!

FOOD FOR THE YORKSHIRE MIND: US LITERATURE

Now tha's ready to launch into us Literature cos its easier reading ner tawking. Start wi us kids' books. Take Snow White and the seven little Sheffield mesters who used to sing "Hay Ho Hay Ho. It`s Off To Work We Go" but now do t'full Monty. The tale goes thusly:

There`s this lass Snow White tha knows wi more brass ner she knows what er do with. Dad`s a millowner i Bradford – clogs ter booits I one generation. Eee cum from muck an thinks ivveryone else stinks but ee knows is tops from is noils so ee`s bow legged wi brass. Ee`s got er name down for Queen Ethelburgas, t`potting shed o`t`Yorkshire rose.

Then er mother pops er clogs, t`mills tekken ower bi Viyella an Dad gets as boozy as a fiddler`s bitch an marries a reet hard faced nattercan. New mum`s got a face like a back end on a bus smash an Snow White gets on er wires cos she`s a reet bit of crackling. So new mum turfs er out.

Work`s as scarce as rocking horse droppings an t`only job the can givver at t`labour is ouse keeper to these seven little mesters I`Sheffield. They`re a comic set, that

Mam sez she'll 'ave Snowie's guts for garters.

bow-legged they couldn`t stop a pig in a passage. When they went t`Epworths ter get some kecks t`tailor sez "Ah`ll never be able ter shape em" ant lad sez "Thee mek em, we`ll bend em". Dead sharp, but then l`Sheffield even t`grass cums up l`blades. They`re not all int`steel. One`s an underground savage an ee don`t mind being bow-legged `cos owt`ll do for t`pit. Another`s ont plonk. Ee`s been redundant that long ee thinks a P45s a revolver. Still they`re a reet `appy lot. Off ter work ivvery day swelting int smelter and Snow White stays at`ome an calls wit neighbours, an cooks their Yorkshire pudden, and she`s as thrng as Throp`s wife when she ung erseen wit`dishclout. She`s as `appy as a pig int`midden.

Then t`step mother enters for t`Daily Mirror Bint ont Year competition an one o`t`little mesters entes Snow White an all. When t`step mother sees t`paper she sez "Mirror Mirror ont`breakfast table which on us is t`most delectable?" An jigger me it`s Snow White. So mam sez she`ll `ave Snowie`s guts for garters. She writes t`t`Hire Purchase company an t`tally man teks TV back, an mam gets their Provident Cheques stopped an mam writes t`t`government an gets t`little mesters nationalised. So they`ve as much brass as a toad as feathers an Snow White`s no job. Ant' little Mesters nawthur cos when the'try ter addle a living stripping like lots ov other Sheffield chuffs t`crowd bells out "Gerrem back on agin". Until the' gets a part in't' film 'T' Full Monty. But it wor only a little part 'cos dwarves 'ave nohhot little pants.

So tha knows poor old Snowie 'as to go ont`game to addle her brass. Then she meets this bloke as runs a Discothick an a Jag. Ee sets er up for a bit ont`side. So she teks misfortune liggen dahn. Till she gets up t`spout an ee as ter marry er. They didn`t live `appily ever after. But this int a Fairy Story. Ee warn`t no Fairy an she weren`t Fairy Snow.

Or there's the great poetry of John Hartley and, is sad lamentations on t'state ov t'poor which once looked dated but don't now wi't'Job Seekers Allowance (the same as calling t'pension t'Death Seekers Allowance). Try Bite Bigger Billy, or Hartley's "Hawpoth."

Wheer is thi Daddy doy. Wheer is thi mam
What are ta crying for poor little lamb?
Dry up thi peepies pet, wipe thi wet face
Teears on thi little cheeks seem aht o'place
What do they call thi lad? Tell me thi name
Have they been oonin thi? Why it's a shame
Here, tek this hawpny an buy thi some spice
Rocksticks or umbugs or summat ats nice
Then run off hooam ageean fast as tha can
Thear. Tha'art allreight ageean. Run like a man

He wiped up is teers wi is little white brat
An ee tried to say summart, Ah couldn't tell what
But is little face breetened wi pleasure all throo
Eh its cappin sometimes what a hawpeny can do

Sob Sob Sob. But Yorkshire poetry isnt just sentimental. It also has a unique insight into God's mind. As in Fred Brown Weyver's vision

When mi weyvin cares
Ha fligged
Content, but fain
Ah'm ligged
On mi daisy patch
O'lawn
Viewin wi new
In-seeing gaze
Mi lupins tall
An all ablaze
Lahk Kessmus cannles
An liggin theer
Ah hear an know
T';Owd familiar
Threat an thraw
Fra Natures bloom
An twig at theas
Breet ends
Cloise raddled wi
Mi awn
Are weyvin theer
A smock Ah's weear
When tahm meeans
Ivvermoar.

There's acres of Yorkshire literature out there. But first finalise speykin so that tha can ask for what tha wants at t'Yorkshire Dialect Society book and recipe shop

SUMMAT TER SAY I'YORKSHER

First test your tonsils to see if they have structural weaknesses or may be warn out by our hard consonants. Say this test piece fifty times

As war bahn down us snicket when t'pictures wor loosin
It were black as us coil oil an mucky as t'tip
I saw t'rag an boan man all brussen wi boozin
Tweltin t'osses ower t'eads wi is whip

The translation is less important than the tonsorial tension but it means roughly that I was making my way down a narrow passage as the pictures were exiting when it was extremely dark and there was dirt underfoot.   I saw a scrap metal merchant, somewhat the worse for drink, and he was belabouring his less than trusty steeds about their heads with his whip. I promptly reported him to the RSPCA.

OK.   Now you've mastered that you need a few phrases to keep up the conversational flow. The kind of things people say to each other just to bridge gaps though they're not quite as polite in Yorkshire. If we say nowt there's nowt worth saying. Ours isn't a language for filling spaces or saying summat for t'sake o'nowt.

Summat to Speyk

Yorksher's a colourful language because we boil everything down to essentials. Here's a sample of Yorksher wit and wisdom about folk which may seem rude and crude to you but compliments in Yorkshire are as rare as bacon flavoured crisps at a synagogue. We're trying to help folk improve themselves. So don't say anything nice to a Yorkshire lass or you may have to carry her home where normally she'd carry you if she's at all interested. Now us sayings. They're pretty direct. But then if someone nivver did nowt for nobody, they're Lancastrians.

We have a lot about meanness because of our dealings with the Scots who pass through on their way not to spend their money in London and don't leave any of it here either. They even haggle over the price of a half litre of petrol on the A1and have been known to buy Seabrook crisps in ones and twos on the grounds that they're not staying in Yorkshire long.

Some illustrations:

Ees that mean eed split a current in two
Ees that tight ee won`t let is teeth chatter when ee freezes
Ees that mean ee wouldn`t pee on yer if yer war on fire
Brass tekken out o`t`pocket is near spent
Ee wouldn`t part wi`t`reek of `is own muck

For restlessness try:

As fidgety as a fly in a bottle
Buzzing about like a blue arsed fly

For laziness:

As idle as a Ludlam dog at leans its ead agint wall ter bark
Ees that idle ee thinsk manual labour`s a Spanish socialist
There`s more work in a Beecham`s pill

To encourage friendly relations with young ladies (never be complimentary):

Does ter bang like t`shit ouse door?
Tha`s as thin as a yard o` pump watter

For clumsiness or awkwardness:

Like orse muck, allus int road
As awkward as Dick`s at band at went nine times round an wouldn`t lee
As awkward as a rail out
As handy as a duck wi a muck fork

For someone who talks too much:

More rattle than a can o` mabs
Tha talks like an alfpenny book baht leaves
Tha knows some clog iron

A sex maniac can be:

As leet geen as a posser head
As leet geen as a lodging house cat

And the really stupid is:

Ten pence t`t`shilling (A Nexercise: Decimalise this)

Ee couldn`t it t`barn door sat ont`sneck
If is brains were dynamite they wouldn`t blow is cap off
Two sandwiches short of a picnic
Ee asnt t' sense to come in out o' t`rain
As daft as a brush
As thick as two short planks
Ee war gotten in slack watter
Look in 'is een.There's no winders oppen (alternatively nobody 'ome)
If tha put is brains in a bee it'd fly backwards.
Ee's dead but ee don't know enough to ligger down
Ee couldn't pout watter out of 'is booit if t'instructions were on t'eel.

Some of these phrases can be understood outside Yorkshire where they are more needed.

Finally here`s a useful collection of phrases to drop in so as to disguise any slight imperfections in your grammar:

Thi mam wants thi booits for loaf tins. *You have big feet.*

Tha couldn`t organise a piss up in a brewery. *I am not impressed with your competence.*

She`s as straight up an down as a yard of pump watter. *Her bust is not well developed.*

Thas as edgy as a crocodile in an andbag factory. *You seem nervy.*

She looks as if she tossed a sparrer an lost. *She shouldn`t wear mini skirts.*

Ee`s a face like a busted clog. *He`s not Omar Sharif.*

Yer don`t look at t`mantlepiece when yer poking t`fire. *I am far from being so ungallant as to complaint about my wife`s looks.*

Ee`d eat t`oven door if it were buttered. *He seemed hungry.*

She`s got one eye on`t pot an another on`t chimney. *She squints.*

Ee`s fine as a fart wi a frill on. *A little overdressed.*

Well, there it is. There are lots more. But you`ll have to go for us course in Advanced Tyke talking to master them all.

Vocabulary

Here is the basic Yorkshire vocabulary on which you'll be able to get by with the addition of some words I'm not able to print here for security Weslyan reasons. You'll probably come across others in which case write them down. The Yorkshire Dialect

Society offers vouchers for meals at Harry Ramsden's for the discovery of any words not at present in its files. However I should warn you that the reward is not proportionate to the amount of money you'll have to spend on drunken old toss pots in the Dales or deepest Barnsley to get them to talk and even if you do they're usually slurred to incomprehension. Though some see that as part of the charm.

ACKERS
: Money. As an object of great veneration in Yorkshire money is honoured by having more words to describe it than any other object. See also brass, dosh, gelt, bunce, megs.

ADDLE
: Earn as in "addle a living".

AGATE
: Get going.

ALE
: Beer. Up here we toast it this way:
"Oft tha`s made me friends mi foo.
Oft tha`s made me pop me cloas
But noa that thas so near me nose
Up that comes an down tha goas"

ANENT
: Next to.

ATE
: To eat "Summat to ate" is a meat pie, not the time of day.

AXE
: To ask, witness the title of the famous question master on Calendar Commentary, Druit the Mad Axe Man.

BACKSLAVER
: Cheek.

BAHN.
: Going. The Germans copied this for their word "Bahnhof" - "do you come here often".

BAHT
: Without. It`s thy round. Nay ah`m baht.

BARMPOT
: Daft.

BELT
: To hit. Yorkshire is rich in synonyms for this act of necessary correction such as twelt, thrash, fetch `im `one, flay, bray, thump, wallop, hammer. Frequent applications are necessary for Southerners, wives and children, particularly other people`s, but the Heckmondwike Novelty Co. will shortly be marketing an aerosol twelting can. Huge export sales to Northern Ireland are forecast.

BEVVIED

*Bevvied = boozed up,
or "three sheets t't'wind"*

Boozed up or plea of extenuating circumstances for bashing, gang bashing etc. The richness of the Tyke tongue is shown by the large number of words for this state of Euphoria such as "three sheets t`t`wind", "drunk as a fiddler`s fart," "canned up," "cut," "losaked," etc. You ask at the Batley Working Men`s Club. They`ve seen em all, even folk with such a skinful it`s running out of their lug holes.

BINT   The low Yorkshireman is deeply religious but his trinity is brass, birds and booze (middle Yorkshiremen are unitarian and believe only in brass). As a major part of this trinity birds are treated with great veneration before marriage. After they`re kept in t'scullary So we have a great variety of synonyms such as bird, lass, Judy, etc.

BLEAR   Smear

BLEARY   Vision when beery

BLETHERED   Whacked

BLETHERING   Conversation of Southerners, Bletherskite, light conversationalist.

BOOZER   Pub. Enter with the gay cry of "Do you serve alcoholic beveridges here?" Note that beer costs at least 20p less than in the South.

BRANT   Steep.

BRAT   Someone else`s child.

BUMBAILIFF   Rent collector. Sad to relate the Mitchell Great, Great, Great Grandfather, Red Bill Sutcliffe, was bumbailiff to Colonel Akroyd of Boothtown. His uniform now sits in Akroyden Museum. Now few Urban District Councils provide uniforms preferring their men to blend in with the background so as not to attract violence.

BRUSSEN   Stuffed. Fit to burst. Also lucky.

CAG (or cack-handed)   Left-handed

CALL	To talk, converse, chat with. Usually used of women since they are allowed to talk among themselves and usually in derogatory fashion.
CAP	To surprise.
CAUSER	Causeway
CHUFF	Daft, except in Sheffield where it's a term of exasperated endearment because so many people are.
CLAGGED	Sticky
CLAHT	Dishcloth.
CLAMMED	Thirsty and hungry
CLOUTHEAD	Daft.
COLLOP	Slice.
DOFF	Take off. As used in stripclubs.
DON	Put on. As not used in stripclubs.
DRUFFEN	Drunk. A drunken man is often compared with Canute.
DYKE	Lesbian. Yet it would be dangerous to assume that Black Dyke had anything to do with a lesbian negress.
EE,EEN	Eyes. "I`ll wall thi `een up" is not a compliment.
ELBOW GREASE	Effort.
FAFFING	Messing about. Not to be confused with pfaffing – sewing.
FETTLE	Clean. My grandmother fettled t'door knocker until it weren`t there any more. She used more pumice stone ont`door step than Etna put out in a decade.
FLAYED	Frightened.
FLIBERTYGIBBET	Blatherskite, lightweight, Southerner.
FLUMMOXED	Puzzled.
FRAME	Shape yourself, manage, try.
FRATCH	Fight, argue.
FRIT	Frightened – as used by Mrs. Thatcher.
GALL ACES	Braces.
GANSEY	Sweater, pullover, jersey

GAPE, GAWP	Stare.
GILL	Half pint. In the South a quarter pint.
GINNELL	Narrow passage way. A snicket baht t`top. Ginnells begin at Baildon Moor. In Sheffield gennell. Elsewhere entry.
GOB	Mouth. But Gobby means daft.
GORMLESS	Stupid, slow, Southerner.
GUMPTION	Produced only I`Gumption Factories all ower Yorkshire. Not found outside.

In Yorkshire proper few words begin with H.

HOBGOB	Simpleton, Southerner.
HUGGER	Carry.
HUMMER	Curse. As in" Bloody Hummer " or "dash it."
KAG HANDED	Left handed, also Keggy handed
KALIED	Drunk. Another term for which there are many synonyms given its close relationship to that central part of the trinity Booze, Sloshed, Pissed, Cut, Fresh.
KECKS	Pants
KNACKERED	Whacked, exhausted.
LEET	Light or to like.
LIG	Lie down. In Silsden they`re a bit lazy cos the only place to go is Steeton and no-one would want to go there. So when the brand new Vicar, Rev. Sidebotham, went to visit an old lady parishioner he was naturally told by the neighbour "She`s gone to liggerdown". " Oh yes, and did the dear lady take the bus or the train?" he said.
LOLLOP	Sprawl
LOOSING	Ending, breaking up.
LUG	Ear.
LUMMOCK	Daft
MARRIED LIFE	Testicles. As in "I`ll ruin yer married life".
MAUNGY	Sulky

MEG	Halfpenny.
MIDDEN	Dunghill or old fashioned earth lavatory. Some people were said to be so lucky if they fell in it they'd come out smelling of roses.
MUCKMENT	Rubbish, Southerner.
MYTHERING	Whittering
NAB	Steal, grab.
NACKERS	Cods, testicles, nuts.
NEB	Front of a cap.
NESH	Cold
NITHERED	Very cold. A condition found on the kind of day that affects brass monkeys adversely.
NOBBUT	Only.
NOWT	Opposite of owt. If it warn't for summat there'd be nowt.
ON	Engaged in, as in on the game, on the job, on the piss.
PAWSE	Kick. "Must give us pause". (Shakespeare)
PAY	Pea. Pay Cloise – pea field. Daft as a pay cloise - Southerner.
PETTY	Lavatory. In Humanby a new vicar went to visit a local family – to their embarrassment. Mother lectured her four sons on the need to speak proper for the occasion only to have George announce as she served dinner "Gie us a lollock o lean an a lollock o fat while ah gan tit'petty". Despairingly she turned to the Vicar "Ahm reet sorry. They an't as much manners as mi arse".
PIGGIN	Lading can.
PIKING	Not paying your round. Very common in Barnsley.
POSHING	A hiding. So a reet poshing isn't going up in the world.
PROGGING	Gathering firewood for 5 November.

Progging = Gathering firewood for Plot Neet

RAZZLED	Burnt
REEK	Smoke
RIG	Back. As ter ever ugged a poak up a stee till thi rig warked?
ROAR	To cry. In Stocksbridge Eli watmough`s wife had just died. Joe his friend went round to sympathise. "Ee ahm reet sorry". "Aye" says Eli "have been roaring all morning an when have ad me dinner ahm going to roar again".
SAM (or sammer)	Pick up, collect.
SETPOT	Clothes boiler. Copper
SGONA	Meteorological term as in Sgona rain.
SHUTTANCE	Riddance
SILING	Pouring with rain. Siling i`stair rods.
SITHA	Look. Fred Trueman debased this to sithee as in "Ah'll sithee" - a usage officially condemned by the Yorkshire Dialect Society`s adjudication panel which funtions in Yorkshire like the Acadamie Francais in France. Fred took bugger all notice.
SLARTING	Spurting. "Ossin ter slart" – "It`s starting to rain".
SLATING	Criticise – slander. Sometimes pour with rain.
SLAVVER	Dribble (but not football).
SLUFFENED	Upset.
SNEK	Door fastening.
SNICKET	Narrow passageway, ginnel.
SPARROW FART	Dawn. I have never heard this rare sound. Nor was it recorded by Ludwig Koch.
SPICE	Sweets.
STARVED	Frozen. Or hungry as in "Ah`m that starved me belly thinks mi throat`s cut, roughly translated as "Is tea ready?"
SUMMAT	Position of great importance. The nicest thing people can say about you is "Ee is summat". Thus: "If tha`as nowt tha`art nowt. If tha`d `ad owt tha`d a been summat". Not to be confused with summat meetings of great powers which are not about owt.
SUP	Drink.

TAWS	Marbles.
TEEM	Crowded, teeming wi folk.
THEE	Like tutoyer in France: Tha thee's them as thee`s thee
THRONG	Crowd: eg "thronging wi folk" or very busy eg "Throng as Throp`s wife when she hanged hersen wit`dishclout".
THROSTLE	Sparrow. Bingley is known as "throstle nest" God knows why.
UPTSPOUT	Pregnant.
WARK	Ache as in Backwark, Bellywark or Bellywak
WARPHEAD	Dimwit, Southerner. Warphead is the beam on the warp weaving loom.
WHILE	Until. Tragedy struck on a new crossing in the North Riding which carried the sign "Do not cross while red light is on".Huge queue formed and poured over while the light was red.
WITTER	Natter in "Lancashire-Maether"as in Maether Macree.
WORRIT	Natter away at something.
WOSSACK	Fool.
YAR	In Bradford "your" but in Huddersfield "our" a situation which has led to a lot of confusion at Rugby League matches when advice is proffered on who should have a girder hacked off.
YAM	Home

That`s it. Tha`s graduated AGYBNQ. Almost as good as a Yorkshireman. But not quite. So a Yorkshire toast which we'll give you for free at the end of this naturalisation course. Repeat after me, raising your glass and buying one for me too:

Er's tiv us – an all on us – an me an all.
May we nivver want nowt, nooan on us.
Nor me nawther!

Think on!

Tha's graduated AGYBNQ -
Almost as good as a Yorkshireman but not quite.

Other Titles from

G R E A T -Ⓝ-O R T H E R N

include

Arthur Ransome and the World of the Swallows & Amazons

Dales People at Work

Farm Yarns

The Great Yorkshire Celebrity Cookbook

Hannah Hauxwell: The Common-sense Book of a Countrywoman

Sand-pilot of Morecambe Bay

Sandwalker

The Two Way Guide to the Settle Line

The Tale of the Mouse

TV Country Favourites

The Yorkshire Dales: A Landscape Through Time

**For further information on these or forthcoming titles
please call Great Northern Books on 01943 604027.**